KEEP
OUT!

TOP SECRET PLACES
GOVERNMENTS DON'T WANT
YOU TO KNOW ABOUT

HIGH-SECURITY FACILITIES, UNDERGROUND
BASES, AND OTHER OFF-LIMITS AREAS

KEEP
OUT!

NICK REDFERN

New Page Books
A division of the Career Press, Inc.
Pompton Plains, N.J.

KEEP OUT!
EDITED AND TYPESET BY KARA KUMPEL
Cover design by Howard Grossman/12E Design
Printed in the U.S.A.

Images on pages 12, 22, 42, 48, 69, 79, 131, 147, 155, 162, 180, 198, and 200 © Nick Redfern. Images on pages 15, 166, 171, and 228 © NASA. Image on page 63 © U.S. Air Force. Image on page 75 © Wikimedia Commons. Image on page 84 © USGS. Images on pages 94, 110, 111, and 192 © U.S. Government. Image on page 132 © U.S. Department of Energy. Image on page 211 © U.S. Navy.

To order this title, please call toll-free 1-800-CAREER-1 (NJ and Canada: 201-848-0310) to order using VISA or MasterCard, or for further information on books from Career Press.

The Career Press, Inc.
220 West Parkway, Unit 12
Pompton Plains, NJ 07444
www.careerpress.com
www.newpagebooks.com

Library of Congress Cataloging-in-Publication Data
Redfern, Nicholas, 1964-
    Keep out! : top secret places governments don't want you to know about / By Nick Redfern.
        p. cm.
    Includes bibliographical references and index.
    ISBN 978-1-60163-184-8 -- ISBN 978-1-60163-642-3 (ebook)
1. Parapsychology. 2. Unidentified flying objects--Government policy. 3. National security. 4. Defense information, Classified. 5. Government information. 6. Conspiracies. I. Title.

BF1040.R42 2012
001.94--dc23

2011036968

For Ken Gerhard, a great friend and seeker of the strange.

ACKNOW LEDG MENTS

I WOULD LIKE TO OFFER MY VERY SINCERE thanks and deep appreciation to everyone at New Page Books and Career Press, but, particularly, Michael Pye, Laurie Kelly-Pye, Kirsten Dalley, Kara Kumpel, Gina Talucci, Jeff Piasky, and Adam Schwartz; and to all the staff at Warwick Associates for their fine promotion and publicity work. I would also like to say a very big "thank you" to my agent, Lisa Hagan, for her constant great work and support.

CONTENTS

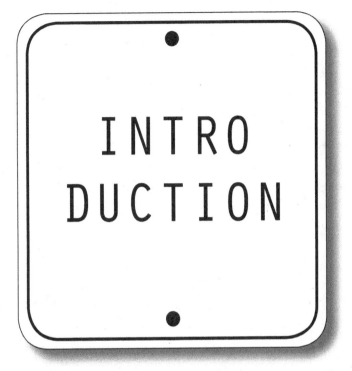

INTRO DUCTION

AREA 51, HANGAR 18, MONTAUK, PINE GAP, Fort Detrick, Rudloe Manor, Zhitkur, Porton Down, the Dugway Proving Ground, and the Dulce Base: These are just a handful of the many highly classified installations of which the governments of the United States, Australia, China, Russia, the United Kingdom, and elsewhere prefer we, the general public, remain steadfastly ignorant. Those governments have extremely good reasons for wishing us to remain in the dark. It is at these secret facilities that, for decades, clandestine research is said to have been undertaken into lethal viruses, genetic manipulation, crashed UFOs and deceased alien entities, biological warfare, mind-control experimentation, futuristic aircraft and spacecraft, teleportation, weather-modification, invisibility, time travel, and much, much more of a conspiratorial and cosmic nature.

Whether situated deep under the oceans, far below the ground, or within the heart of hidden, remote desert locales, these super-secret places are guarded with paranoid zeal by those in power who wish to keep their secrets buried and locked far away from prying eyes. Sometimes, however, the huge, steel, near-impenetrable vault-like doors that help to hide the truths open wide—or are forced open—and the shocking secrets within are revealed...

C - 1

THE ULTIMATE SECRET BASE

WE HAVE TO START SOMEWHERE ON OUR QUEST for the truth about top-secret sites, so it seems appropriate that our attentions should first focus upon the most infamous of all classified installations. Can you guess its name? I strongly suspect you can.

It all goes back to 1989, when a man by the name of Robert Scott Lazar went public with a series of sensational claims that continue to reverberate to this day. A self-admitted maverick scientist, Lazar asserted that for a brief period of time in the late 1980s he was employed in a scientific capacity at an incredibly secret, well-protected installation situated in the harsh wilds of the Nevada desert. The program to which Lazar had been assigned was, he said, one of astonishing proportions and profound implications: a clandestine operation to evaluate, comprehend, and ultimately duplicate an impressive fleet of spacecraft of nonhuman origin that had, quite literally, fallen into the hands of the U.S. government—or, perhaps more accurately, into the sweaty palms of an elite scientific body of officialdom that quite possibly was not answerable to the presidential office. Yep, you read it right: According to Lazar, behind closed doors, watched over 24/7 with a *Shoot first and don't even bother asking questions later* attitude, Uncle Sam was intensively researching real-life, honest-to-goodness flying saucers—and maybe even their extraterrestrial crews as well. Thus was born, or was exposed, the legend of Area 51.

Without doubt the definitive secret base, Area 51 is an installation composed of a mass of huge, impenetrable hangars, mysterious underground chambers, and winding, labyrinthine tunnels. The idea that such a place could at the same time be both classified and widely recognized might sound like the ultimate oxymoron, but it happens to be absolutely true. The U.S. government steadfastly—and somewhat ridiculously, given that practically everyone has heard of it and knows of the alien rumors—refuses to discuss the specific nature of the Area 51 facility.

Just the Facts

Before we get to Lazar and his alleged UFOs, let's first take a look at what we *can* say with certainty about this particularly intriguing installation. Despite Area 51's reputation as some sort of remote fortress buried far, far away from civilization, it most certainly is not. The

Area 51: The ultimate secret base.

surprising reality is that the base is located less than 90 miles from the glittering lights, spacious hotels, countless slot machines, and gyrating strippers of Sin City. What makes Area 51 so impenetrable—to the vast majority of people, anyway—is not its distance from Las Vegas, but the extent to which its innermost secrets are maintained.

Try piloting a plane over the base's strictly enforced no-fly zone and you risk being blasted out of the sky by a missile. See what happens if you decide to take the highways and byways to the base: You'll soon find yourself watched closely by humorless, Men in Black–style private-security goons who, if you fail to heed the signs and stark warnings to turn back, will be only too happy to make life extremely difficult for you. Significant monetary fines, several months of jail time, and even the use of deadly force may be invoked to deter you from making an exciting road trip with your buddies into the desert in search of E.T. Given that such security extends for literally miles outside of the perimeter of Area 51, it's little wonder that—just as is the case with its glitzy, money-draining near-neighbor—what happens at Area 51 is forever destined to stay at Area 51. At least, most of the time. Just occasionally—to the chagrin of officialdom—some of Area 51's many cans of worms spill open into the public domain.

In terms of what the base's name implies today—in short, aliens—"Area 51" is a relatively recent phenomenon; it extends back only a little more than two decades. In terms of the base's actual existence and its secret workload, however...well, that goes *way* back; more than half a century, even. And it's called Area 51 for a very good reason: Rather than being a solitary, stand-alone facility, Area 51 is actually just one of a number of areas on the Air Force's vast Nevada Test and Training Range that, in total, extends to more than 4,500 square miles.

Just to the northeast of Area 51 is the sprawling dry lakebed known as Groom Lake, where, during the hostilities of the Second World War, practice bombing missions were secretly undertaken. Come the 1950s, by which time the Soviet Union was already the next big threat to the Western world, the CIA very quickly (and very secretly) got in on the Area 51 action. As a result, by 1955, a huge 5,000-foot runway was constructed at the base, from which CIA test flights and landings of the super-classified U-2 spy plane were successfully conducted. As both time and aviation-based technology progressed, so did the clandestine programs at Area 51.

When the 1950s became the 1960s, the SR71 *Blackbird* aircraft became a staple ingredient of the research, projects, and missions at Area 51. Then, in the late 1970s and throughout the 1980s, base personnel were engaged in perfecting the so-called Stealth technology that became so famous when, in 1988, the U.S. government revealed to the world the latest addition to its military arsenal: the Stealth F-117 *Nighthawk*. To demonstrate the depth of the secrecy that surrounded Area 51's involvement in the development of the *Nighthawk*, we now know it had secretly been flying missions as far back as 1983—and provoking more than a few notable UFO reports in the process—even though the 80s were nearly over when the world's media was finally shown the strange-looking, angular, utterly black aircraft. This leads us to Area 51's cosmic reputation as the U.S. government's very own top-secret saucer-central.

Lazar's Revelations

Robert Scott Lazar—Bob to his pals—is a figure who, when it comes to UFOs, has quite possibly caused more headaches for American officialdom than anyone else on the planet. Whether that is because Lazar has successfully blown the lid off a conspiracy of otherworldly proportions or because he has spun an elaborate web of fantasies that the government is constantly forced to deny remains to be seen. But whichever way the coin falls, the story is a humdinger, to be sure.

It was an otherwise normal evening in March 1989 when the cosmic shit hit the fan—with unrelenting force. As the unsuspecting citizens of Las Vegas turned on their televisions at dinnertime to watch KLAS-TV, they could have been forgiven for thinking it was April Fools' Day. (Some might say they were not so far off the truth.) But let's not jump the intergalactic gun: They saw a man on TV telling an amazing story to an investigative journalist named George Knapp. The slim, 30-ish, bespectacled speaker was Bob Lazar, but you would not have known it then—at the time (as a result of serious worries for his personal safety, he claimed), Lazar was going by the alias of Dennis. So as the good folk of Sin City sat and listened, Dennis/Lazar claimed that in late 1988 he had been recruited as a physicist into a Top Secret research and development program out at a particular section of Area 51 called S-4. He said it was an intense R&D effort that focused on nothing less than the analysis of nine captured, donated, or otherwise acquired spacecraft from other worlds. The craft operated on fantastically advanced technological principles, and Lazar had seen the evidence for himself.

Despite warnings and less-than-veiled threats from Area 51 personnel to never, *ever* reveal what was afoot at the mysterious base, here was Lazar doing precisely that: spilling the beans to the world at large. As a result, his life was under threat of termination. With the alien secrets tumbling wildly out of Lazar's mouth, a government-wielded Sword of Damocles was ready to fall upon him at any moment. His tale of an alien conspiracy and extraterrestrial power systems in the hands of the government was a newsperson's dream story. It was Woodward and Bernstein for the space age. It was what UFO researchers the world over had waited for so long to hear. But was it true? Simple question; not-so-simple answer.

Who Is Bob Lazar?

Bob Lazar is a character as enigmatic as he is intriguing. Some members of ufological circles view him as a crusading hero, and others view him as an outrageous fraud. Let's start with the facts: Born in Florida in 1959, Lazar is known to have taken courses in electronics at the Los Angeles–based Pierce College in the 1970s, and to have spent some time employed with Fairchild, a company founded in 1959 by Nobel Prize–winner and co-inventor of the transistor, William Shockley. But that's only part of it. Lazar claimed—and *continues* to claim—that he received an MS in electronics from the California Institute of Technology (Cal Tech), and an MS in physics from the Massachusetts Institute of Technology (MIT), and also that he worked on some pretty classified stuff in the process.

In 1982, we find Bob splashed across the front page of the New Mexico–based *Los Alamos Monitor* newspaper, in a lengthy article that detailed his skills in relation to one of his personal passions: building and racing super-fast jet-cars. The article described how Lazar and a NASA friend hauled the engine out of an otherwise innocuous Honda, and then did something pretty remarkable: They replaced the old engine with a new one made of stainless steel and titanium that burned liquid propane, allowing for speeds close to 200 miles per hour—pretty much the automobile equivalent of mutating Dr. Bruce Banner into the Incredible Hulk. The article showed that Lazar certainly does have brains and technical savvy, but what's particularly notable about it is that it specifically detailed the hero of the hour as being a physicist then working at the Los Alamos Meson Physics Facility. Today known as the Los Alamos Neutron Science Center, the facility has long been at the forefront of cutting-edge research into particle physics. So, despite the fact that Lazar has been dismissed as a hoaxer or fantasist, we have at least some evidence that he *was* plugged in to the secret world of the highly classified Los Alamos facility, approximately six years before he allegedly began tooling around with alien saucers at Area 51. But how does one go from unleashing super-fast Hondas on the world and earning a wage at Los Alamos to getting the lowdown on the biggest secret of all? It was all due to fate; a chance, life-changing meeting.

In June 1982, legendary theoretical physicist Edward Teller gave a lecture at Los Alamos, and Lazar attended. As Lazar approached the venue on the day in question, he was amazed to see Teller sitting casually outside on a wall, reading the aforementioned *Los Alamos Monitor* article on Lazar himself. This was highly fortuitous, so Lazar introduced himself and had a brief chat with the man who was one of the inspirations for the deranged Dr. Strangelove in Stanley Kubrick's classic 1964 movie of the same name.

Lazar's Introduction to Area 51

Now let's fast-forward to 1988. At that time, Lazar was running a photo lab in Las Vegas, but was on the lookout for far more gainful employment. He sent out a resume to Teller, who remembered Lazar and his beefed-up Honda. This was very good news. It got even better when Teller agreed to use his contacts to see about getting Lazar back into the world of physics. As a result, Lazar was approached by a representative of Edgerton, Germeshausen, and Grier, Inc. (EG&G), a U.S. defense contractor. Thus began a strange saga filled with many a cloak, dagger, and hall of mirrors.

After interviewing at the EG&G offices at Vegas's McCarran Airport for a job he was quickly deemed way overqualified for, Lazar was pleased to be called back, for a different potential position. This one was reportedly focused on something that was vaguely explained as an advanced propulsion-based project—surely an understatement of mammoth proportions. The fact that, at the time, Lazar had his very own particle accelerator in his bedroom was enough to impress his interviewers. They made an offer, and Lazar quickly accepted the gig. Things were moving forward. Just how far forward, Lazar had no real idea. He soon found out, however.

Lazar was met at EG&G by a mysterious man named Dennis Mariani, described as being military-like, stern, and to-the-point. Mariani would become Lazar's immediate supervisor. They took a brief flight, followed by a short drive in a bus with blacked-out windows, to Area 51's inner sanctum: S-4. Lazar was about to graduate

Hiding Nevada's UFOs.

from playing with jet-cars to handling craft that, he was told, originated from the depths of another solar system. The location where the alien ships were being held and studied was appropriately out-of-this-world too: The S-4 facility was said to be just like something out of a James Bond movie. Lazar claimed it was composed of a number of buildings and large hangars that, rather than being built in the open, were actually sculpted right out of the rock of one of the huge mountains that dominated the area. To help camouflage the mysterious installation and protect the dark secrets hidden deep within, the huge outer doors were spray-painted in a sandy color that blended in quite naturally with the surrounding desert landscape.

Initially, things were pretty intense for Lazar, who was still unclear about the precise nature of the program to which he had accepted a position, beyond the fact that it was shrouded in secrecy, sounded seriously intriguing, and was maybe somewhat off-the-wall. Upon arrival, Lazar quickly became acquainted with the fine spirit of teamwork at Area 51 and S-4: He was forced to agree to have his home telephone monitored, and was made to sign a security oath that included a clause to the effect that, upon accepting the position, he agreed to waive all his constitutional rights as an American citizen. The outrageous intensity didn't end there: Threats were made, guns were pointed, and there were warnings about the use of sophisticated drugs and hypnosis to silence those on the project who failed to toe the line. Lazar was even monitored by an armed guard when he had to go to the bathroom. What was going on? Now was the time for the ace to be played, for the UFOs to finally be unveiled.

It's not every day that someone invites you to examine a fantastically advanced vehicle designed and built on another world. But Lazar was hardly your average guy, and he embraced the challenge eagerly. And it wasn't just one such craft that Lazar knew of, but nine. Whether they were obtained as a result of malfunctions, crashes, or generous donations from the aliens themselves, Lazar never did find out. But regardless of how they got there, they *were* there, laid out before him in the secret hangars of S-4; a veritable armada of flying saucers of the precise type that the U.S. government had for decades officially assured the general public were merely the stuff of fantasy, hoaxes, and misidentification.

Lazar's time at S-4, destined to be brief, was twofold: Part of it involved him digesting numerous briefing papers on the nature and history of the aliens' mission on Earth. The bulk of his job, however, was focused on trying to understand and ultimately replicate the power source of the amazing craft—which was reportedly a super-heavy element not found on Earth called Element 115. The ships themselves were strange: All utterly smooth to the touch and circular in shape, they completely lacked nuts, bolts, and rivets, and looked as if they had been extracted right out of molds. They were compact in size, split-level, and did not exactly make for comfortable physical navigation—that is, unless you were a 3-foot-tall alien, as the intelligences behind the craft were reputed to be. From the briefing papers Lazar learned that the project indeed had more than alien craft in its possession: there were extraterrestrial bodies that had been secretly autopsied too. Furthermore, there had been violent, fatal altercations at Area 51 between *living* alien entities and U.S. military personnel at the base. The briefs led Lazar to believe that the human race was the result of some sort of alien-initiated genetic tinkering in our ancient past, and, perhaps most ominous of all, E.T. seemed to have an interest in the nature of the human soul.

The biggest problem for the surprisingly small body of personnel assigned to the program—maybe 20 at most—was that the successful duplication of Element 115 on our world was simply not feasible given the level of scientific knowledge at the time. As a result, much of the investigation was trial and error, undertaken by personnel who understood the implications of what they were dealing with, but were not necessarily sure how to deal with it. Significant advances were few and far between. Try to imagine a Neanderthal kicking the back tires of a shiny new Corvette and grunting the caveman equivalent of "Hmmm." That, basically, was the situation Lazar found himself in at S-4. Nevertheless, a few tentative test flights of a couple of the craft were attempted at a very restricted level in front of the hangars, so, clearly, at least some degree of headway had been made.

Bob Spills the Beans

Lazar asserted that he continued working at the base until the early months of 1989, around which time a couple of critical things occurred that ultimately led to the termination of his employment—and perhaps almost to the termination of his life. Despite all the warnings, threats, and intimidation about not discussing his work with anyone outside of Area 51 and S-4, Lazar chose to do precisely that: He quietly told his wife, Tracey, his good friend, Gene Huff, and UFO researcher John Lear—the son of William Lear, of Lear-Jet fame—of the startling secrets hidden at the base. Bad move.

It was too much to hope that Area 51 security personnel would not find out. *Of course* they found out. They also learned—as a result of their constant monitoring of Lazar's home telephone—that while Bob was tinkering with alien spaceships at S-4, Tracey, who was taking flying lessons at the time, was secretly tinkering with her flight instructor. Lazar was duly informed of his wife's affair, and also that his employers knew all about the revelations he had made to his pals Huff and Lear. It was these two issues that led Area 51 staff to quickly revoke Lazar's security clearance, amid worries about his psychological state and the attendant security risks. Lazar was summarily kicked out of his job, and slung out of Area 51. Adios, aliens.

Shortly afterward, Dennis Mariani telephoned Lazar and demanded that he return with Mariani to Area 51. Fearful that, having violated his security agreement, his bones might very well end up buried in the Nevada desert if he did so, Lazar flatly refused Mariani's hostile invite. An irate Mariani slammed down the phone on Lazar. Not long after that, someone shot out one of the back tires of Lazar's car as he proceeded onto a particular stretch of Vegas highway. Whether this was a failed attempt to kill Lazar or merely a carefully orchestrated means to intimidate him into complete silence remains unclear. But Lazar felt it left him with only one viable option: He had to go public.

In Lazar's mind, the more visible he became, the less likelihood there was of him disappearing at the hands of government assassins. Thus began the revelations on Las Vegas's KLAS-TV, followed by endless debate on the veracity of Lazar's story in various books, magazines, television documentaries, radio-based talk-shows, and—more than 20 years later—all across the Internet.

what is the truth?

Essentially, that's the story. But what are the facts? *Are* there even any facts in this weird saga? Or is it all a bunch of lies and distortions? The answers to those important questions are all dependent upon whom you care to ask, and how you interpret the available evidence. Many UFO researchers and investigators dismiss Lazar's revelations with barely a second glance. Nuclear physicist and legendary UFO authority Stanton T. Friedman wrote of Bob's revelations, "THIS IS PURE BUNK. BUNK.

BUNK."[1] And yes, Friedman *did* put his statement in all caps! But despite the naysayers, whenever an attempt is made to place Lazar's assertions firmly in the categories of hoaxing and delusions, something always seems to come along that leaves the hangar-door open—or, at the very least, slightly ajar—and offers a degree of support for Lazar's sensational story.

Let's go back to the beginning, to Lazar's claims that he was offered the job of a lifetime as a result of having approached Dr. Edward Teller. When questioned after the murky matter began to take shape within UFO research circles as well as the mainstream media, Teller did not deny having met Lazar. Nor did Teller deny having referred Lazar to additional sources that may ultimately have led him to Area 51. In fact, Teller actually squirmed, with distinct uneasiness apparent in his voice, manner, and appearance, when he uttered the following words, after being put on the spot by an enterprising television journalist: "I probably met him. I might have said to somebody I met him and I liked him, after I met him, and if I liked him. But I don't remember him."[2] Right, Edward, that really clarified matters.

And what about those qualifications Lazar claimed to possess? No convincing evidence of any sort has ever surfaced in support of Lazar's claims to have obtained degrees at Cal Tech and MIT. Critics and debunkers gleefully rub their hands together and cry: "Foul, Bob!" Lazar's response? The government is trying to discredit him by erasing significant portions of his background and life history. On the other hand, it might reasonably be argued that the lack of credible data pertaining to Lazar's educational assertions would be enough to rule out the possibility of his ever having been considered for employment in the world of government-funded, cutting-edge science.

Lazar's claims to have worked at Los Alamos were also disputed, and viewed with suspicion by certain elements of both the UFO research community and the mainstream media. In fact, his claims were outright refuted by spokespersons of Los Alamos itself. For a short while, at least. Soon, something came along that turned that issue on its head: KLAS-TV's George Knapp found Lazar's name in the October 1982 telephone directory of the Los Alamos National Laboratory. When the evidence was presented to grim, red-faced Los Alamos officials by Knapp, they quickly chose to modify their position. The new version of events was that Lazar *had* been employed by them after all, but under the umbrella of an outside contract company called Kirk-Meyer. They maintained that Lazar never, ever, not even once, worked on issues of a secret or sensitive nature. However, colleagues of Lazar had informed Knapp that Lazar worked at Los Alamos on matters relative to the highly sensitive Strategic Defense Initiative (SDI)—or "Star Wars" program—that had been grandly envisioned by President Ronald Reagan in the 1980s.

What of those claims about fantastically advanced craft at Area 51 supposedly fueled by a super-heavy element that cannot be found on Earth (Element 115)? Here we have to turn to the strange story of a young Welsh man named Matthew Bevan, who, in the mid-1990s, doggedly set out to crack the UFO secrets of Wright-Patterson Air Force Base's so-called Hangar 18. This got the teen terror into scalding hot water with both British and American authorities. Bevan's full story will be told in due course in a later chapter; as a small section of it relates to Lazar, however, it's vital that we note it here. One part of Bevan's experiences—recorded officially by Scotland Yard during the course of its series of interviews with Bevan immediately after his 1996 arrest—focused upon him hacking his way into files and systems at Wright-Patterson that appeared to describe a craft astonishingly similar in design to one of those outlined by Lazar to George Knapp, even down to the super-heavy-element angle. Does that mean Lazar lives to fight another day?

As Bevan told it, on one particular system at Wright-Patterson that he accessed he came across a stash of e-mails in which there was a discussion about some sort of radical aircraft being developed at the base. It was described as very small and split-level, with a reactor at the bottom and room for the crew in the top section. When Scotland Yard's Computer Crimes Unit asked Bevan if he saw anything else on the Wright-Patterson computers, he replied that yes, he did: He saw classified information on an anti-gravity propulsion system powered by a heavy element. The cops then wanted to know if Bevan had downloaded any of this information, printed it, and then secretly circulated it to colleagues within the UFO research field. Bevan assured them—at least three times—that he had not. The vehicle Bevan described to Scotland Yard sounds very similar to those to which Lazar claimed secret access at Area 51.

The Third Possibility

Even if Lazar is telling the truth as he saw it, does that necessarily mean we can trust his version of events? That might sound like an odd question, but, beyond the issue of whether Lazar is a teller of fantastic truths or a purveyor of outrageous lies, there is that third possibility I alluded to earlier. It's one that is very seldom considered: Perhaps Lazar faithfully related to George Knapp (and later to many others) what he was told about and saw at Area 51, but Lazar was himself utterly lied to about the real nature of the "UFOs" to which he was exposed. What if the vehicles weren't actually from another world after all? What if they were just the latest in a long line of amazing, futuristic craft developed and built at Area 51 by a team of technical wizards employed by good old Uncle Sam? What if the E.T. angle was introduced as a convenient cover to mask the terrestrial truth?

Aurora

UFOs and aliens aside, it is a fact that Area 51 has a long and secret history of designing, housing, and test-flying radical, unusual-looking aircraft. Mention has already been made of the U-2, the *Blackbird*, and the *Nighthawk*. But those babies are nothing when compared to a craft that has become legendary within both ufological and mainstream aviation circles. Its name, supposedly, is *Aurora*, and it officially does not exist. It is rumored to be a large, triangular, highly advanced aircraft able to fly almost silently. It is said to be capable of performing astonishing maneuvers, such as hovering for significant periods and traveling at tremendous speeds high in the upper atmosphere. The *Aurora* has been spotted in the skies of our world more and more often since the 1980s. Thus was born the mystery of what has become known as the Flying Triangles.

One stunning incident that may be relevant to the *Aurora* controversy occurred late at night in central England on March 31, 1993. The location was a military base in the English county of Shropshire called the Royal Air Force Shawbury. The primary witness was the base's meteorological officer, a man named Wayne Elliott. What he saw was a gigantic, triangular-shaped object flying at a height of no more than 200 feet, and only about a similar distance from the base's perimeter fence. Bearing in mind that a meteorological officer would generally be considered a highly reliable witness, well-trained in recognizing numerous types of aerial phenomena, we have to conclude that Elliott was able to accurately judge the size of the object, which he estimated to be somewhere between that of a C-130 *Hercules* and a Boeing 747 *Jumbo Jet*. Elliott also reported that the craft gave off a highly unpleasant low-frequency hum, and at one point fired a beam of light down to the ground that tracked very rapidly back and forth, sweeping one of the fields adjacent to the base. Then it suddenly shot away at a fantastic speed, leaving the meteorological officer staring, awestruck, into the night sky.

Even the nation's Ministry of Defense sat up and took notice of this event. Many people, including one of the Ministry's official investigators of the affair, a man named Nick Pope, concluded it was due to the actions of visiting extraterrestrials, but others cast their suspicions in the direction of Area 51 and *Aurora*. Pope admitted that when the Ministry's investigation of the incident was at its height, he and his colleagues could not ignore the various rumors that were making the rounds about a supposed Top Secret aircraft developed by the U.S. government called *Aurora*—or, indeed, *any* hypersonic prototype aircraft operated by the Americans. Questions were duly asked, but the only response from the United States was this: There is no such aircraft as the *Aurora*, nor is there any craft even remotely similar to what Elliott claims he saw.

Is it possible that the United States military was being somewhat economical with the truth when replying to the Brits? Let's look at the words of one Walter Bosley, or, as he used to be known, Special Agent Walter Bosley, of the United States Air Force Office of Special Investigations. Bosley, now retired from the world of officialdom, has gone on the record as stating that while working on counterintelligence programs from 1994 to 1999, he was involved in the secret circulation and dissemination of bogus UFO stories to act as convenient covers to hide and protect the test flights of advanced, terrestrial aircraft utilizing Stealth technology. Some of these craft were the secret developments of McDonnell-Douglas and Lockheed. As long as the UFO faithful believed these craft had alien origins, and continued to pursue this false angle, officialdom was pretty much happy, as it kept the pesky, meddling saucer-watchers away from investigating secret, high-tech projects of a distinctly human nature.

Could it be that this is also what happened at Area 51 with Bob Lazar? Was everything he saw a charade?

Lazar believes not, and suggests that one of the key arguments against such a scenario is that it's wholly implausible to imagine that the permanent stabilization of Element 115—or, as it's officially known, Ununpentium, an incredibly heavy element in the periodic table—could be achieved on Earth. In 2004, however, Russian scientists from the Dubna-based Joint Institute for Nuclear Research, along with U.S. colleagues at the Lawrence Livermore National Laboratory, reported that they had achieved very brief synthesis of Element 115. Can we, therefore, completely rule out the possibility that someone else has secretly achieved long-term synthesis? If so, perhaps they did not originate in some far-away galaxy, but from Nevada—at Area 51's S-4.

spy Game

It is a matter of historical record that, particularly from the mid-1980s onward, when the Air Force—by its own admission—illegally grabbed nearly 90,000 acres of open Nevada land as a means to further restrict public access to Area 51, Russian spies were quietly checking out the area, attempting to bribe base personnel into spilling the secrets of what was *really* going on at that mysterious installation. There were serious concerns, acknowledged openly by Walter Bosley, that members of the UFO research community might be clandestinely exploited by the Russians as a means to uncover the truth about the United States's secret-aircraft programs.

Gerald Haines, a historian of the National Reconnaissance Office, said, with respect to CIA involvement in UFO investigations in the 1980s, "Agency analysts officially devoted a small amount of their time to issues relating to UFOs. These included counterintelligence concerns that the Soviets and the KGB were using U.S. citizens and UFO groups to obtain information on sensitive U.S. weapons development programs (such as the Stealth aircraft)."[3]

In that case, there might very well have been a great deal of motivation for Area 51 staff to briefly hire a somewhat maverick character like Lazar to act as the fall guy for an elaborate scheme in which they expose the man to what he is led to believe are alien craft. Because they had done background checks on Lazar and his character, they could guess that he would probably be unable to resist talking about such monumental issues, so they wait patiently until he decides to go public. But maybe Lazar doesn't talk quite as quickly as the S-4 guys might have anticipated or preferred, so they initiate a mock assassination attempt to speed things up—one that was never intended to physically harm Lazar at all, but was certainly designed to scare the you-know-what out of him, and ensure that he quickly went running to some outfit like KLAS-TV. Then, the alien story is out, wildly circulating among the media and the UFO research community, and there's no turning back.

Then, with tales of UFOs at the base circulating here, there, and everywhere, Area 51 security personnel sit back and wait to see if anyone named Boris or Ivan starts poking their noses around, attempting to bribe both Area 51 employees and UFO researchers with links to the aviation industry as a means to learn more about what's afoot at Area 51. Then, like a spider moving in on a fly, American agents quickly pounce. Boris and Ivan have been ingeniously lured into a complicated web as a result of Lazar's revelations, arrests have been made, and—here's the most important issue of all—*no* legitimate secrets have been compromised in the process.

So in this theory, the saucers were not alien craft, and the revelations of Lazar were not accurate. But the attempts of the Russians to learn the secrets of Area 51's super-classified aircraft—such as *Aurora*—were all too real, and the U.S. government's real secrets were successfully protected by a complex UFO-themed smokescreen. That the Russians may have been foiled by a brilliantly executed plan involving spurious data on UFOs, aliens, and extraterrestrial technology, with the involvement of Bob Lazar—quite possibly the biggest unknowing patsy since Lee Harvey Oswald himself—is, in many ways, even stranger and more sensational than the notion that Area 51 might really be home to nine crashed (or donated) UFOs from a world far, far away.

It is important to note that even Lazar himself admitted that, while he was at S-4, the base personnel played "so many mind games there."[4] Those five words—which probably remain unappreciated by most that have followed his story—just might have been Lazar's most revealing words of all.

Then again, perhaps Lazar really *was* speaking the literal truth from the very beginning: Maybe, while the gamblers are systematically drained of their dollars and the strippers bleed dry those who prefer to spend their money in more entertaining ways, as the bright lights of the city forever flash with a hypnotic allure in downtown

Las Vegas, fewer than 100 miles away, those nine flying saucers still sit in that classified base known as Area 51, their amazing secrets known only to a select few—one of whom, just maybe, for a brief time in the late 1980s, was Robert Scott Lazar.

C - 2

CLOSE ENCOUNTERS OF THE UNDERGROUND KIND

DURING THE EARLY 1950s, MY FATHER, Frank Redfern, served with the British Royal Air Force as a radar mechanic, and was involved in a series of extraordinary UFO incidents that occurred throughout the course of three days and nights during the latter part of September 1952. The encounters took place at the height of a military exercise code-named Mainbrace, and involved a number of fast-moving, unidentified targets that were tracked over-flying the North Sea by radar operators at RAF Neatishead, Norfolk, England, for several days. The aerial encounters mystified the finest minds of the Air Ministry's scientific and technical personnel.

When my father related this story to me I was barely 13 years old; it proved to be a key turning point in my life and ultimately led me on a continuing quest to determine the strange truth that lies behind the UFO puzzle. I made mention of my father's experience in my first book, *A Covert Agenda*, which hit the bookstores in late 1997. Following its publication, a number of important sources came forward to corroborate the remarkable events of September 1952—including a man named Bill Maguire, who had enlisted in the Royal Air Force in 1950. To say that Maguire had an interesting story to tell of a Top Secret facility is quite an understatement.

Bill Maguire

For a brief period in September 1952, at the height of Operation Mainbrace, Maguire was holed up in a Top Secret military facility buried far below the English countryside. It was hardly of conventional proportions: The entrance-point was a metal hatch that sat atop a small mound in the middle of a normal-looking field near RAF Sandwich, in the county of Kent. Maguire was afforded a truly astonishing, firsthand taste of just one of many government-controlled underground lairs that secretly dominate the world below our very feet. As he lowered himself into the entrance-point, Maguire was confronted by a staircase that descended for approximately half a mile into a huge room populated by more than a hundred people, all frantically involved in tracking something sensational on the huge wall of radar screens that dominated the room.

As Maguire finally got his bearings within this massive underground domain, and as the situation was revealed to him in its starkest form, the reasons behind the blind panic became staggeringly clear. It seemed that some form of absolutely gigantic UFO was being tracked on the radar scopes high above the deep waters of the English Channel, and, as a specialist in radar, Maguire's thoughts, analyses, and conclusions about what was afoot were immediately required. But, then, without any warning, something astonishing occurred: The gargantuan UFO split into three sections, all of which proceeded to zoom away at phenomenal speeds. One section went north, a second headed towards the French coastline, and the third was tracked until it finally disappeared in the Eastern Balkan region. Afterward, Maguire said, he was told by the superior officers present never to talk about the strange series of events, and he did not for almost half a century. (Whatever it was that Maguire, and a whole team of experienced radar operators, tracked from that vast, secret underground complex nearly 60 years ago, it is to Maguire's credit that he eventually had no qualms about speaking out publicly.)

Aside from what may have been occurring in the sky all those years ago, what to make of the extraordinary world that Maguire encountered far below the surface? Can we, today, identify it? The answer is yes; or, at least, with near certainty we can.

By 1949, the tension that existed between East and West was worsening, and a catastrophic, civilization-ending atomic confrontation between the Soviet Union and the United States was seen by many as being right around the corner. As a result, deeply concerned British authorities recognized it was imperative that preparations should be made to deal with the unthinkable, should such a terrifying situation ever come to pass. As a result, a highly secret program was launched by the British government to create a brand-new chain of radar installations throughout the country, with a significant number located on the eastern and western coasts. The classified program became known as Rotor, and it led to the careful construction of a wealth of secret bunkers that, in a national emergency involving a confrontation with the Russians, would work diligently to defend the nation from outright nuclear disaster.

One of those installations that played a significant role in Rotor was none other than the aforementioned RAF Sandwich. During the hostilities of 1939–1945, the base was termed a Ground Controlled Interception site. It was located at Ash Road, in the town of Sandwich (after which the base was named) and was comprised of nearly 400 active personnel. Eventually, however, its operations were transferred to a secret, below-ground, two-level installation in the nearby village of Ash. The Ash installation was not completed until May 1953, with operations commencing there in August 1954. However, there seems to be very little doubt that the classified bunker to which Bill Maguire was taken, from which the movements of the extraordinary aerial object were tracked (and which he clearly recalled was located somewhere extremely close to RAF Sandwich), was, at the very least, *somehow* inextricably linked to the secret Rotor program. To what extent the staff hunkered down in the Rotor bunkers may have tracked UFOs on other occasions is unfortunately unknown. But there is an interesting footnote to this particular matter and the saga of Bill Maguire.

Specifically commenting on the extraordinary underground complex to which Bill Maguire was taken via a hidden entrance in an innocuous-looking field near RAF Sandwich in 1952, the late Graham Birdsall of *UFO Magazine* had the following to say: "As recently as 1997, I learned how Communications Technicians were operating from supposed disused airfields and similar mothballed bases here in the UK, whose location and means of access to underground facilities below must remain confidential. However, I can categorically state that one such access point was described as being in the middle of a plain-looking field."[1]

Could it be that this is a direct reference to the underground installation to which Bill Maguire was dispatched all those years ago? If the answer to that question should be yes, then it may well be the case that to this day its deeply buried staff still continues to secretly monitor the skies for UFOs. And apparently, it's not the only British-based underground installation with a Top Secret tie to the UFO conundrum. That's right: There are more.

Rendlesham Forest

Between the nights of December 26 and 28, 1980, a series of almost science-fiction-like events occurred in Rendlesham Forest, Suffolk, England, a densely treed area adjacent to the joint Royal Air Force/U.S. Air Force military complex of Bentwaters-Woodbridge. Essentially, what many believe took place throughout the course of several nights was nothing less than the landing of a craft from another world, out of which small, humanoid entities reportedly emerged. The vehicle was tracked on radar, deposited traces of radiation within the forest, succeeded in avoiding capture, duly made good its escape, was the subject of intense secrecy on the part of both British and American authorities...and thus created a wild controversy that rages to this very day.

Equally profound are the rumors suggesting that far below the now-decommissioned installations exists a super-advanced base, possibly with an intimate connection to the UFO mystery. One of those who has commented at length on this particularly mysterious underworld is a man named Larry Warren, a U.S. Air Force witness to the UFO landing at Rendlesham Forest in December 1980. Warren, at the time a member of the Air Force Security Police, has stated that his own, personal encounter occurred late on the night of December 28. It sounds just like something straight out of *Close Encounters of the Third Kind*. Warren's experience was hardly Hollywood fiction, however; it was incredible, unearthly fact.

Is there a huge installation below the now-decommisioned RAF Bentwaters, England?

As the evening unfolded, rumors flew around the base about the nature of the UFO encounters of the previous two nights. Military personnel armed with sophisticated scientific equipment and hardware were reportedly swarming around the dense, dark woods, seemingly anticipating the return of the UFOs. Wild animals, such as deer and rabbits, were seen fleeing the forest in unbridled terror, clearly spooked to their collective cores by something menacingly unknown in their midst. And, at the height of these extraordinary events, Warren and a number of his colleagues and friends were ordered to head into the heart of those spooky woods. As for why? Well, they were just about to find out.

The mystified group carefully made its way through the trees, until a clearing was finally reached, on the other side of which was an open expanse of field...which, ominously, seemed to be illuminated by a form of weird, glowing fog. The tension began to mount. As Warren and his colleagues slowly moved closer, they could now see there were already approximately 40 personnel in the field, some armed with cameras, others weighed down with sophisticated motion-picture equipment, and a few even possessing Geiger counters.

The reason *why* suddenly became graphically and unbelievably clear: From the direction of the North Sea, a small ball of red light came flying towards the unearthly fog, and then stopped, hovering right above it. In an instant, there was a blinding flash. When Warren's eyes acclimated to the situation, he could see that both the ball of light and the fog were now completely gone. In their place was something even more remarkable: At a distance of only about 20 feet from the shell-shocked Warren and his comrades was a pyramid-shaped craft that was clearly mechanical in nature, and appeared under intelligent control. That sight was nothing compared to what happened next, however.

A large ball of bluish-gold light appeared from the right side of the UFO, and moved slowly away from the craft, to a distance of about 10 feet from the stunned airmen. Within the ethereal ball were three entities; three non-human intelligences from some unknown realm. *Aliens.* The ball then split into three cylindrical creations, each containing one of the three beings, which were attired in silvery suits, had large heads, and displayed large, cat-like eyes. They weren't locals, then. According to Warren, some sort of communication—possibly telepathic—took place between the creatures and a high-ranking U.S Air Force officer, after which Warren and his colleagues were ordered to return to their trucks and await further orders. And that's precisely, perhaps somewhat reluctantly, what they did. The encounter in the woods, for Warren at least, was over. But there was something even stranger waiting on the horizon for him, something destined to take the man not back into Rendlesham Forest, but *under* it.

It was maybe 6 p.m. on the following night when Warren, on-base but by then off-duty, received a telephone call. The mysterious voice on the line gave no indication of his identity, but ordered the bemused Warren to be in the dorm parking lot in 20 minutes, where he would see a dark blue sedan waiting for him. From his icy tone, the man might as well have added "Or else," just for good measure. All the while wondering what was going on, Warren followed the orders like a good soldier, and sure enough: there was the car, waiting to take him to destinations unknown. He was motioned to the back door of the sedan by two silent men in dark suits—the dreaded Men in Black, perhaps—and got in the car. But something was wrong; something was *very* wrong. An eerie, green glow suddenly filled the vehicle, and a strange feeling overcame Warren. Somehow rendered into a semi-conscious, befuddled state, and unable to speak clearly or move properly, Warren later speculated that perhaps he had been secretly drugged in some unfathomable fashion. Regardless of how such a situation was achieved, Warren was now as helpless as a terror-stricken deer caught in high-beam headlights.

The next thing Warren recalled, in his semi-sedated state, was being taken to another location, followed by what he described as a definite descent that affected the pressure in his ears. The inference was clear: rather than being taken back to base, Warren was now being trans-ferred to somewhere deep beneath it. With his mind al-tered and his body unable to fight back, Warren's involve-ment in whatever was about to happen next was pretty much assured. Through his stupor he saw rooms filled with high-tech equipment and computers, and was mo-tioned towards a massive door. He walked through it on distinctly unsteady feet, and found himself in a darkened room, to the left of which was some sort of opening, ac-cess to which was prevented by a Plexiglas window.

"I stepped into the confined area and felt as if I was no longer on Earth," Warren later recalled. "I found my-self looking into a gigantic, dark, cavernous space. It re-minded me of the interior of the Houston Astrodome in a strange way. Beads of humidity rolled down the other side of the seamless glass."[2] Notably, Warren also recalled seeing a craft resting in a corner of the huge installation, looking very much like the one he had encountered in Rendlesham Forest the previous night. Lights he saw in the distance, Warren was informed by those carefully guiding his movements, represented a huge tunnel under the base that led out to the cold waters of the North Sea.

Warren was then directed to a large, translucent screen, through which he could see the shadowy silhouette of a small-sized, living entity, although it was impossible to make out any specific physical details. But there was something very strange and undeniably unearthly about the creature, or whatever it was: Warren began to sense words and imagery in his mind, all of which gave every indication that the being knew intimate, personal details of Warren's life and character. The creature also informed Warren, again via some form of mind-to-mind contact, that it originated within a realm of existence that Warren would never be able to comprehend.

Notably, further data was imparted to Warren by the unknown entity in front of him to the effect that he was indeed in a secret facility far below the base, that the underground installation had existed since the 1940s, and was expanded upon in the 1960s, thus allowing the creature and the rest of its kind access to the facility via the huge tunnel system that reportedly had both entry and exit points approximately a mile off the coast of the town of Lowestoft, Suffolk. Warren was also advised that other such secret bases existed across the entire planet; their purpose, however, was never quite made clear.

"Larry: In your life, strive to remember," were the final words that filled Warren's head, before the entity vanished, and Warren succumbed to oblivion and the arms of Morpheus. When he finally, slowly regained his senses, Warren found himself back on the surface, wandering around the regular RAF Bentwaters base, in somewhat of a daze. To his shock and concern, it quickly became apparent to Warren that no less than two days had passed since his strange, underground experience began. Now, more than 30 years on, Warren *still* does not know what to make of the odd events that occurred deep below RAF Bentwaters; only that, in his own words, "I left part of my soul somewhere underground."[3]

Rudloe Manor

There is one final secret installation in the United Kingdom worthy of study when for its reported UFO connections. As with the story of Larry Warren, it is a place filled with secrets, both above and below the ground. The rumors that have been bubbling quietly but continuously within certain factions of the British UFO research community since at least the late 1970s is that the relatively innocuous-looking base known as Royal Air Force Rudloe Manor, situated within the county of Wiltshire, sits atop a large, futuristic, underground installation, deep inside of which resides the holiest of all ufological prizes: alien bodies from a crashed UFO.

British authorities have long asserted that the stories are all nonsense; little more than modern-day folklore and mythology in the making. Determining the truth of this seemingly endless affair has proven to be just as problematic as the base is deep. One thing that can be said with certainty, however, is that the area of Wiltshire in which Rudloe Manor is situated is the source of a rock

RAF Rudloe Manor: a real-life underworld.

known as *Bath Stone*, which has been quarried extensively for many years—hence huge underground openings, caverns, and tunnels that certainly *do* exist deep beneath Rudloe Manor and throughout certain sections of the immediate, surrounding countryside.

Until 1998, the Royal Air Force's elite Provost and Security Services (P&SS) had their headquarters at Rudloe, and their duties included the investigation of crime and disciplinary matters involving RAF personnel, the vetting of employees, and the issuing of identity cards, passes, and permits. Far more significant is the fact that investigators attached to the P&SS are also trained in counterintelligence (C/I).

Such training is undertaken at the RAF Police School. Prospective candidates for counterintelligence work are required to take specialized courses in subjects such as computer security and surveillance. Before being considered for C/I work, personnel have to attain the rank of corporal within the RAF Police. C/I investigators are responsible for issues affecting the security of the RAF, which can include the loss and theft of classified documents, matters pertaining to espionage cases, and the protection of royalty and VIP's when visiting RAF stations.

Also situated within the headquarters of the P&SS is a division known as the Flying Complaints Flight, which primarily investigates complaints of low-flying military aircraft in Britain. In addition, on October 17, 1996, a member of the British Parliament, Martin Redmond, who had a personal interest in the UFO puzzle and was fully aware of the rumors linking Rudloe with aliens, asked a number of questions in Parliament that revealed further data on the workings of the Rudloe installation. Eleven days later, Redmond was informed by then-Defense Minister Nicholas Soames that RAF Rudloe Manor was home to a parent unit and five lodger units. Specifically, these were:

1. The Detachment of 1001 Signals Unit, which operated the British military's communications satellite system.

2. No. 1 Signals Unit, which provided voice and data communications for the entire RAF, Royal Navy, Army, and Ministry of Defense.

3. The HQ of the P&SS.

4. The HQ of the P&SS Western Region.

5. The Controller Defense Communications Network (DCN), a tri-service unit controlling worldwide communications for the military. The

DCN was situated 120 feet underground and was capable of housing no fewer than *55,000 people* in the event of a national emergency.

Soames very carefully refrained from mentioning anything relative to UFOs. So much for the official story.

But what else was, or *is*, possibly going on at Rudloe? Is the base *really* the British equivalent of the infamous Area 51?

In 1987, Timothy Good, a dedicated UFO researcher and author, revealed how, after having been tipped off that something strange—unidentified and flying—was afoot at Rudloe, he visited the base and spent some time strolling around taking photographs. Unsurprisingly, Good was later detained by the local police and asked specifically what he was up to and what his intentions were. Good duly revealed the truth: He had heard the UFO rumors and was determined to uncover the facts for himself. He was later released by somewhat bemused police officers clearly unaware of Rudloe's UFO connection, with a warning to take extreme care when walking around the perimeter of a sensitive British military base in the future.

That was the last UFO enthusiasts heard about Rudloe for a time. In 1991, Timothy Good revealed the account of a former special investigator with the P&SS who claimed specific knowledge of its involvement with UFOs, chiefly with respect to the Flying Complaints Flight. Further corroboration came from a former counterintelligence investigator who informed Good's source that he had access to just about every Top Secret file held there—*except* those relative to low-flying issues; it was his understanding that those files dealt with UFOs. Stressing that he could get in pretty much anywhere at the time, the informant added, "...but not in that department. I remember they used to have an Air Ministry guard in the passage—you couldn't get past them. We could see the Provost Marshal's Top Secret files but yet I couldn't get into the place dealing with UFOs."[4]

In 2000, Rudloe Manor was placed under the control of the Defense Communications Service Agency, which was later replaced by the Information Systems and Services, itself a part of the Ministry of Defense's Defense Equipment and Support organization. A few of its underground areas have since been sold off, and some are now decommissioned. Notably, other areas, extending to significant depths, remain solidly in the hands of officialdom, and are out of bounds to just about everyone else.

$$\bigcirc$$

The British government's UFO secrets, it appears, are deemed important enough to be held under lock and key at all times—whether at secret facilities like RAF Rudloe Manor, or possibly within fantastic, cavernous underworlds of the type to which Bill Maguire and Larry Warren were taken, in September 1952 and December 1980, respectively. As in *The-X-Files*, when FBI Special Agent Fox Mulder was most keen to stress that "The truth is out there," perhaps we should amend those now-famous words to: "The truth is *under* there."

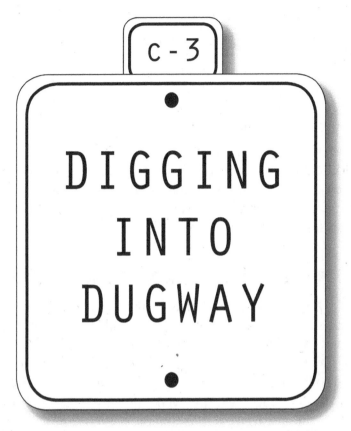

C - 3

DIGGING INTO DUGWAY

IN THE LATTER PART OF JANUARY 2011, AN event described as a serious mishandling of a highly toxic nerve agent led to the temporary but complete lockdown of a Top Secret facility deep within the deserts of Utah. For a tense (but fortunately brief) period, the nation's media reported on the mysterious affair, until assurances came from officialdom that all was well, everything had just been a big misunderstanding, and the good folks of the Beehive State were not about to be infected by some nightmarish cocktail conjured up in a dark underground lab.

We will return to this particularly controversial story in good time, but before we do so, we have to first go back to the dawning of the 1940s, when that same Top

Secret facility—known today as the Dugway Proving Ground, or DPG—first reared its head.

Located 85 miles from Salt Lake City, the enormous DPG sits squarely within Utah's Great Salt Lake Desert, and is shielded by a huge expanse of mountains that dominate the landscape. Its creators chose their location well—but not quite well enough to avoid attracting publicity, controversy, and even outrage on more than one occasion.

A History of chemical warfare

One of the unfortunate side effects of the human race's advancing technology is the ability this technology gives us to kill each other. Such is the case with the development and potential usage of extremely toxic substances that may be derived from living organisms: a.k.a. biological and chemical warfare. Make no mistake: The history of chemical warfare is long and dark. For example, during the First World War, from 1914 to 1918, German forces unleashed a terrifying onslaught of mustard gas upon unsuspecting Allied troops at Ypres, Belgium. The result: thousands of agonizing deaths under truly horrific circumstances. Sarin gas has also proved to be a cold-hearted player in chemical-warfare tragedies: In 1995, numerous people were injured and 13 died when Sarin vapor was released into the winding depths of Tokyo's underground rail system by the apocalypse-obsessed Aum Shinrikyo cult—an event that briefly plunged Japan's capital city into chaos as people scrambled to flee the jammed tunnels of death. Chemical warfare, then, is a highly dangerous game.

Death Needs a New Home

Prior to the early years of the Second World War, the U.S. military was pretty much reliant upon the expertise of the Army's Aberdeen Proving Ground in Maryland for researching, understanding, developing, and offering protection from chemical-warfare agents. The biggest problem for military strategists of the time was that Aberdeen was hardly remote, let alone inaccessible, to theoretical invading hordes. After all, its northernmost tip practically sits on top of the Chesapeake Bay. So, to ensure that the United States's research programs into chemical warfare could advance in a place that would offer personnel—as well as their deadly creations—protection from potential hostile nations and foreign spies, plans were made to build a new installation situated far away from prying eyes, in an area as remote as it would be secured.

Thus, on February 6, 1942, President Franklin D. Roosevelt signed off on an order giving the War Department complete control over an astonishing 126,720 acres of previously open, public land, and the construction of a huge, secrecy-shrouded installation with both above- and below-surface facilities began. The Dugway Proving Ground quickly sprang to life. By the mid-1950s, more than a quarter of a million acres of additional land had been turned over to Dugway officials, thus massively increasing the size and scope of this isolated installation.

Despite various name changes in the years that followed, the mandate of the DPG remained very much unchanged: to further U.S. knowledge in the field of chemical and biological warfare. Today, the DPG has expanded to nearly 800,000 acres, and its airspace is constantly patrolled by the Air Force. And though understanding how the nation might best be protected from the ravaging effects of chemical warfare is without doubt a vital matter, it has not all been smooth sailing at Dugway. Not by a long shot.

Dead Sheep in Skull Valley

Imagine if you can a stark and shocking scene: It is early in the morning in mid-March 1968, and you are a rancher in Utah's Skull Valley, a Native American Indian reservation of the Ghoshute tribe, less than 30 miles from the Dugway Proving Ground. Your income is mostly derived from breeding and selling sheep to the local communities, so your daily routine is to carefully nurture, feed, watch over, and house your animals. But this particular morning is destined to become one quite unlike any other. In fact, it's about to turn into an absolute disaster.

As you ride your trusty steed (or drive your all-terrain vehicle) to the usual grazing area of your flock, you are met by a shocking sight: As far as the eye can see, sheep are lying dead on the valley floor. Others are struggling to take their very last breaths. Some wobble around on unsteady legs, their fates already tragically sealed. A few lie on the ground, unable or unwilling to move, suffering from fatal internal hemorrhaging. In the days to come, the casualty figure rises to 1,000 sheep. Then to 2,000. Finally it reaches a number that exceeds 6,000. To the uninitiated this may sound like the opening scenes of a big-bucks Hollywood eco-thriller. It is not. Rather, it represents one of the most notorious events in the history of the Dugway Proving Ground.

It became clear very quickly to those who called Skull Valley and its immediate surroundings their home that something deadly and disastrous had occurred in their midst. Even before the evidence was in, the locals were looking in the direction of Dugway—and *only* in the direction of Dugway. History has demonstrated they were wise to do so: On March 13, 1968, mere days before the sheep deaths occurred, personnel at Dugway had secretly engaged in several open-air tests using an agent known as VX, a chemical weapon that, today, is officially classed as weapon of mass destruction, and the use of it is banned by the United Nations. Utterly odorless and tasteless, VX makes for the ideal weapon: By the time a person even realizes that something is wrong, he or she may very well already be on an excruciating one-way road to oblivion. And that, as the people of Skull Valley learned at the cost of their livelihood, goes not only for human beings, but for sheep too.

When the scale of the tragedy became clear, the news spread like wildfire—or just like VX. On March 16, 1968, the panicked manager of a livestock company in Skull Valley breathlessly telephoned a Dr. Bode, who was then attached to the University of Utah but working under contract to the DPG, and informed him of the discovery of the sheep's bodies. Quickly and astutely recognizing the likelihood of a connection to the activities of the nearby Proving Ground, Bode, in the early hours of March 17, called the chief of the Ecology and Epidemiology office at the DPG to report the initial deaths. As more and more reports swarmed in to the heart of Dugway, the realization that an event of disastrous proportions had occurred was fast becoming undeniable.

Well, to some it was undeniable; not to others. Outrageously, instead of owning up to their cataclysmic errors, staff at the base initially had the gall to place the blame on the ranchers' use of organophosphate pesticides on their crops. That is, until autopsies of some of the sheep, chosen entirely at random, revealed the presence of levels of VX that were certainly significant enough to account for all of the deaths. Staff at the base was then forced to take a second look at the grim picture.

Secret reports and studies were duly prepared—all of which remained classified for years, and in some cases for *decades*—which clearly and undeniably implicated the DPG, and no one and nothing else, in the sorry state of affairs. Ranchers in the area were financially reimbursed by the government for the loss of their livestock, but there was still a great reluctance on the part of the DPG to officially own up to anything at all.

This would not be the only occasion when mysterious deaths of animals in the area were tied to the secret activities of the Dugway Proving Ground. On the Independence Day holiday weekend of 1976, no less than 20 horses were found dead on the Proving Ground, in an area called Orr Springs—precisely where certain germ warfare tests had taken place. Three days later, another 30 were dead. Scott Baranowski, a young soldier who was ordered to the site, helped to bury the carcasses of some of the unfortunate animals, after they had been carefully autopsied by base doctors. Then, quite suddenly, Baranowski fell briefly ill too, with a 104-degree fever accompanied by severe aches and pains.

The Army flatly denied that it had engaged in any sort of outdoor experimentation using nerve agents, and suggested—in extensive reports now in the public domain—that all the horses had died from nothing stranger than thirst, which is highly ironic, given that most of the bodies were found very close to sources of abundant water. In addition, a number of the bodies showed evidence of many large sores, and scientists from the DPG quietly informed Baranowski that some extremely hostile material was then currently being tested on base. Its true nature and origin, perhaps mercifully for us, remains unknown. Collectively, this all led Baranowski to believe that death from dehydration and thirst did not even begin to tell the whole story—maybe *none* of it. Nor did he believe that the lung cancer with which he was later diagnosed was unconnected. To this day, the Army and the DPG vehemently disagree with him.

Human Testing

Baranowski may not have been the only person deeply physically affected by their time spent at the Dugway Proving Ground. Steve Erickson, of the Citizens Education Project of Salt Lake City, who heavily researched the history of the DPG, said that many of the tests run at the base involved human subjects, some of whom were military personnel, and "can only be described as human experimentation."[1] He cited one example in which soldiers were given BZ—a hallucinogen not unlike LSD in terms of its effects upon the human mind. A second example involved a group of Seventh Day Adventist volunteers who were exposed to a swarm of hungry mosquitoes that had been deliberately infected with a biological warfare agent by staff at Dugway as a means to try and determine if such insects could be considered viable methods of delivery.

Lest anyone dismiss such claims as conspiratorial nonsense, it is worth taking into consideration the following quote from an official (and officially declassified) General Accounting Office report of September 28, 1994: "From 1951 through 1969, hundreds, perhaps thousands of open-air tests using bacteria and viruses that cause disease in human, animals, and plants were conducted at Dugway. It is unknown how many people in the surrounding vicinity were also exposed to potentially harmful agents used in open-air tests at Dugway."[2]

Five Aliens in Utah

One of the most controversial aspects of the secret research undertaken at the Dugway Proving Ground is its link to classified matters of otherworldly proportions—UFOs, in popular terms. Shortly before his March 2010 death, one Colonel George Weinbrenner—who held the position of Chief of the Foreign Technology Division (FTD) at Wright-Patterson Air Force Base, Ohio (which is the rumored home of the legendary Hangar 18)—made a six-word statement to his caretaker: "We have five aliens in Utah."[3] He would say no more about it. Granted, this brief statement is open to a fair degree of interpretation, but researcher Anthony Bragalia has suggested his comment may be a reference to the Dugway Proving Ground. And this was not the first time Weinbrenner had spoken outside of official channels about such issues.

In the 1970s, Weinbrenner confirmed to filmmaker Robert Emenegger that highly classified film footage of UFOs was held by elements of U.S. officialdom, but Weinbrenner was concerned about saying too much publicly—namely, what he *really* knew about UFOs. This may have been due to his suspicions of being spied upon by someone in the government. Researcher Anthony Bragalia has noted that this fear of Weinbrenner's may have explained why he always spoke in distinctly guarded terms whenever the matter of UFOs surfaced. When one takes into consideration that (as will become apparent in a future chapter of this book) many of the claims surrounding Wright-Patterson's Hangar 18 demonstrate a close link between its work and that of the base's Foreign Technology Division, it's practically a given that Weinbrenner, as a former head of the FTD, would have had some knowledge of recovered alien bodies and their several areas of storage. And that brings us back to the present day, and the events of late January 2011.

Base Lockdown

It was around 5:30 p.m. on January 27 when the doors to the Dugway Proving Ground were firmly closed and locked. From that point on, no one was getting into the installation—and none of the approximately 1,500 workers on base at the time was getting out. That situation remained in force for nearly 12 hours. Shortly after the DPG went on alert, and as rumors began to circulate that something serious was up, Colonel William E. King IV, the base commander, said that Dugway's staff was doing its utmost to rectify the situation as soon as was humanly possible.

The official reason for the lockdown was given in a brief statement from the Army on January 28: On the previous afternoon, during the course of a regular check of stockpiled items, it was believed that a small vial of the nerve agent VX—the very same substance that killed more than 6,000 sheep back in 1968—had gone missing. In reality, however, nothing had gone missing; apparently the panic was all due to nothing stranger than a labeling error on the vital vial. Maybe that's really all there was to it. Not everyone is so sure, though.

Around the same time that the lockdown occurred, strange lights of unknown origin were seen flitting around the skies near the base. They even became the subject of a major news story on Utah's ABC-4 News. In a segment titled "Strange Lights Appear in the Sky Above Utah County," reporters said the witnesses were clear that whatever they had viewed were neither conventional aircraft nor helicopters. One unidentified flying object even seemed to drop something to the ground. Interestingly, of the various eyewitnesses who agreed to be interviewed by ABC-4 News, one had served in the military, and said that whatever had fallen from the sky was most certainly not a flare or anything so down-to-earth. But just because something is an unidentified flying object, does that automatically mean it is an alien spacecraft?

'Genesis'

For years, rumors have circulated that, as well as testing some deadly nerve agents, the Dugway Proving Ground also test-flies certain highly advanced aero-forms. Dave Rosenfeld, the president of the research group Utah

UFO Hunters, is of the opinion that at least *some* of the many UFO sightings that he and his group have scrupulously catalogued in and around the Dugway Proving Ground for years may be due to the test-flights of radically advanced aircraft. He opines that perhaps the DPG is "the new Area 51," and possibly even "the new military spaceport."[4]

Rosenfeld may not be too wide of the mark. On September 8, 2004, NASA's *Genesis* spacecraft slammed into the desert floor of the Dugway Proving Ground after successfully collecting a sample of charged particles ejected from the sun's upper atmosphere—or what is known as solar wind. The plan all along was for the craft to come down at Dugway, but a big problem with its parachute resulted in the anticipated smooth landing turning into a full-blown *crash*-landing. Not surprisingly, the craft was

Utah's biggest secret: The Dugway Proving ground (where two helicopters are shown here recovering *Genesis*).

significantly damaged, and so was its precious, unique cargo. Fortunately, however, after the area was sealed off (due to a leak of toxic substances from *Genesis'* batteries), a recovery team was able to safely collect the vial containing the particles and transfer it to NASA for careful analysis. The good news was that even though the solar-wind specimens had, to a degree, been compromised as a result of being partially exposed during the crash, NASA scientists were able to make a number of significant breakthroughs with respect to the makeup of such solar phenomena.

⊘

Taking into consideration the curious UFO encounter at the time of the January 27, 2011 lockdown and the combined words of Colonel George Weinbrenner and Dave Rosenfeld, I will leave you with a thought-provoking question: Given that the Dugway Proving Ground is at the cutting edge of classified research into chemical weapons, has been the site of a number of intriguing UFO sightings, and was the spot where one of NASA's own spacecraft plummeted to Earth, is it totally out of the question to suggest that the DPG secretly knows a great deal about somebody else's—or some*thing* else's—spacecraft too?

C - 4

SECRETS OF WORLD WAR II

THE SECOND WORLD WAR WAS SIX YEARS OF carnage that has caused decades of discussion. One particularly tantalizing topic relates to certain secret wartime activities undertaken by the Nazis: namely, the plundering of priceless historical treasures by Adolf Hitler's hordes as a means to fund his war effort, and Nazi Germany's overriding fascination with religious artifacts. What does any of this have to do with the theme of the book you hold in front of you right now, you ask? Quite simply, there is a substantial body of data available suggesting that much of that plundered material, as well as certain unique items of quite literally biblical proportions may, nearly 70 years after the war's conclusion, remain hidden

65

in prominent facilities, including, incredibly, the Vatican and the Smithsonian.

Just like the maniacal Hitler himself, a significant portion of high-ranking Nazis, such as Richard Walther Darré, Rudolf Hess, Otto Rahn, and Heinrich Himmler, had major, unsettling obsessions with the supernatural and the mystical. Rahn, for example, who made his mark in a wing of Nazi Germany's greatly feared SS, spent a significant period of time deeply engaged in a quest to find the so-called Holy Grail, which, according to Christian teachings, was the dish, plate, or cup used by Jesus at the legendary Last Supper. The Grail was said to possess awesome and devastating powers, and the Nazis were desperate to locate it, in order to utilize those powers as weapons of war against the Allies. Thankfully, the plans of the Nazis did not come to fruition, and the Allies were not pummeled into the ground by the mighty fists of God.

Heinrich Himmler, acknowledged by many historians as the driving force behind such research, was, perhaps, the most obsessed with the occult. In 1935, he became a key player in the establishment of the Ahnenerbe, which was basically the ancestral heritage division of the SS. With its work largely coordinated according to the visions of one Dr. Hermann Wirth, the chief motivation of the Ahnenerbe was to conduct research into the realm of religious archaeology; however, its work also spilled over into areas such as the occult, primarily from the perspective of determining whether a particular artifact was a tool that, like the Holy Grail, could be used to further strengthen the Nazi war machine.

Then there is Trevor Ravenscroft's book *The Spear of Destiny*, which detailed a particularly odd fascination Adolf Hitler had with the fabled spear, or lance, that supposedly pierced the body of Jesus during the crucifixion. Ravenscroft's book maintained that Hitler deliberately started the Second World War with the intention of trying to secure the spear, with which he was said to be obsessed—again as a weapon to be used against the Allies. So the account went, however, Hitler utterly failed. Ravenscroft suggested that as the conflict of 1939–1945 came to its end, the spear came into the hands of U.S. General George Patton. According to legend, losing the spear would result in death—a prophecy that that was said to have been definitively fulfilled when Hitler committed suicide.

Perhaps not every ancient artifact remained quite so elusive to Hitler. One rumor suggests that an attempt on the part of the Nazis to locate the remains—or, at least, *some* of the remains—of the legendary Ark of Noah was actually successful. It's a strange and secret story that takes us from the icy-cold peak of Turkey's Mount Ararat to a classified location in one of the United States's most cherished and historic locales: the Washington, D.C.–based Smithsonian Institution.

The Bible states: "God said unto Noah.... Make thee an ark of gopher wood.... And this is the fashion which thou shalt make it of: The length of the ark shall be three hundred cubits, the breadth of it fifty cubits, and the height of it thirty cubits." A cubit roughly equates to 20 inches, thus making the Ark 500 feet in length, 83 feet in width, and 50 feet in height. In addition, it is said that the Ark was powerful enough to withstand the cataclysmic flood that allegedly overtook the globe and lasted for 40 terrible days and nights. As legend has it, when the flood waters finally receded, the Ark came to rest on Mount Ararat.

Exactly *why* Hitler was after the Ark is unclear, but the fact that he *was* hot on its trail is indisputable. Intelligence files generated by Britain's highly secretive MI6 in 1948 state that, in the closing stages of the war, rumors were coming out of Turkey that German military personnel were then engaged in flying a sophisticated spy balloon (based upon radical Japanese designs) over Mount Ararat, attempting to photograph the area. Then, if the operation proved successful in locating the Ark, they planned to recover it—or whatever might be left of it, given the passage of time and the harsh conditions on the perpetually snow-capped mountain.

The Japanese, who were closely allied with Nazi Germany during the Second World War, were indeed master builders of advanced balloons. Arguably one of the best-kept secrets of the Second World War, the "balloon bomb," or *Fugo* as it was generally called, was a classified weapon constructed and flown by the Japanese military. No less than 9,000 such devices were built and employed against the United States. More than 32 feet in diameter when inflated, the balloons were constructed out of paper or rubberized silk and carried below them payloads of small bombs powerful enough to wreak havoc if stumbled upon at the wrong moment. They were intensively launched from the east coast of Honshu during a nearly six-month period beginning in the latter part of 1944, and traveled more than 6,000 miles eastward across the Pacific to North America. The vast majority of the Fugos failed to reach their planned targets, but U.S. Army estimates suggested no less than a thousand made it to the States, the majority having come down in such West Coast states as Oregon, British Columbia, and Washington.

Thus, given what we know about their expertise in such areas, the Japanese may very well have helped their Nazi comrades locate Noah's Ark by providing some form of highly advanced reconnaissance balloon that could be directed over Mount Ararat. Available MI6 files are frustratingly incomplete—maybe *too* conveniently and suspiciously incomplete—and do not reveal whether or not the operation was in any way successful.

Britain's MI6: home to classified files on Noah's Ark.

Mysteries at the Smithsonian

Witness testimony has suggested a fantastic scenario that some see as far-fetched: Certain sections of the famous Smithsonian Institution are off-limits to the general public due to certain unacknowledged archaeological wonders contained therein. Indeed, available data suggests that (in an eerily parallel to the final scenes of the 1981 Indiana Jones film, *Raiders of the Lost Ark*) deep below the Smithsonian there exist secret chambers housing anomalies from humankind's ancient past—perhaps even the fragmentary remains of what was once known as Noah's Ark.

Said witness, an employee of the Smithsonian named David Duckworth, revealed that in the fall of 1968 a number of crates were delivered to the particular section of the Smithsonian to which he was assigned, and provoked a significant amount of interest on the part of senior personnel. The crates contained within them ancient pieces of wood and a selection of very old tools. Possibly echoing—or directly connected to—the story of a Nazi/Japanese balloon utilized to find the Ark, Duckworth stated that the unique stash of material contained photographs reportedly taken from a balloon, and showed a ship-like object partly buried in the ice of a mountainous location. On speaking with colleagues, Duckworth was quietly told that the site displayed in the photographs was Mount Ararat, and the ship in question was Noah's Ark.

Five days later, the excited atmosphere began to change. All discussions of the Ark came to a sudden halt as people were told to keep their mouths firmly shut, and the priceless evidence was gathered up and removed to a new location. Duckworth, after making the mistake of speaking with people outside of the Smithsonian about the Ark rumors, paid an ominous price: he was visited at work by two men who identified themselves as agents of the FBI. The visiting special agents made it clear to Duckworth that his very talkative mouth was making significant waves; he had been somewhere he shouldn't have been, and had seen things he had no business seeing. End of story.

Had the Nazis really found Noah's Ark? Did their Japanese-assisted, balloon-based operation actually work? And did that same discovery somehow, years later, secretly fall into the hands of the U.S. government and the Smithsonian? Even if there *does* exist a secure vault—or series of vaults—at the Smithsonian where such legendary materials are still being maintained and carefully studied, officialdom is today saying nothing of any significance on the matter of that old wooden ship.

Nazi Gold

Here's another important question: If such an ambitious Nazi program to recover whatever was left of the Ark *did* go ahead, then how was it funded? Similar to a lot of the Nazis' unsuccessful efforts to overwhelm the Allies, the funding may have come via controversial means.

As the hordes of Adolf Hitler took on the combined might of Western Europe, the United States, and the Soviet Union, as a means to ensure that its war efforts proceeded at an ever-increasing pace, the behemoth-like Nazi regime came up with a bright idea: They plundered, stole, and confiscated as much gold, treasure, and other priceless items as they could from those nations on whose territory they had left their terrifying marks. They then duly (and secretly) transferred the spoils to certain sympathetic banks (including the Swiss National Bank) in return for hard currency. The stark nature of this massive program was detailed in a document generated by the U.S. government on June 2, 1998, titled "U.S. and Allied Wartime and Postwar Relations and Negotiations With Argentina, Portugal, Spain, Sweden, and Turkey on Looted Gold and German External Assets and U.S. Concerns About the Fate of the Wartime Ustasha Treasury."

Stuart Eizenstat, who served in the Carter administration in the position of Chief Domestic Policy Adviser and under the Clinton administration in the positions of Deputy Secretary of the Treasury and Undersecretary of State for Economic Business and Agricultural Affairs, stated on publication of the report that: "The Swiss National Bank must have known that some portion of the gold it was receiving from the Reichsbank was looted from occupied countries, due to the public knowledge about the low level of the Reichsbank's gold reserves and repeated warnings from the Allies."[1]

Findings suggested that Switzerland had been the recipient of more than $400 million in gold plundered by Nazi Germany. That figure, however, was later upped to around $440 million, as Eizenstat explained: "New sources recently came to light that provided additional information about the infamous Melmer account at the Reichsbank, named after Bruno Melmer, the SS officer who was responsible for taking materials, possessions from concentration camp victims and others at killing centers and depositing them in an SS account in the Reichsbank."[2]

Moreover, $300 million—the equivalent of a stunning $2.6 billion in the economy of 1997—in Nazi gold found its secret way to such neutral countries as Portugal, Spain, and Sweden at the height of hostilities, no less than 75 percent of which was clandestinely channeled via the Swiss National Bank. And there was an even more controversial story to come, involving nothing less than the secretive world of the Vatican.

During the Second World War, the Nazis established what was, essentially, a puppet outfit in Croatia called the Ustashi that was as ruthless as it was relentless in stealing gold and other items of great value from the populace. Around $80 million was secured by the Ustashi for Nazi military programs, some of which, in the latter stages of the war, also reached Swiss banks. Eventually a very big problem surfaced: The Ustashi was reliant upon Germany for financial support, as well as for security and military aid. With the irreversible collapse of the Nazi regime midway through 1945, however, the abandonded Ustashi began to spiral downward into splintered factions and unrelenting chaos. Seeing the end as being well and truly near, its high-ranking officials hot-footed it to Italy, and ultimately got a warm welcome from Rome's San Girolamo pontifical college. It was run by one Father Dragonivic, and almost certainly received significant monetary funding from the Ustashi, possibly even with Vatican assent and knowledge.

On October 21, 1946, one Harold Glasser, the Director of Monetary Research at the U.S. Treasury Building in Washington, D.C., received a Top Secret communication from a certain Emerson Bigelow, an agent of the Treasury. Bigelow wrote that he had learned from a reputable Italian informant that, of the significant funds secured be the Ustashi movement, no less than approximately 200 million Swiss Francs found their way to the Vatican and were held deep within its vaults for safe-keeping. According to further intelligence data, Bigelow added, a significant percentage of this amount may have been secretly dispatched to Spain and Argentina via a Vatican pipeline. Bigelow conceded, however, there was a possibility this was merely a carefully arranged cover story, and that the vast sum may never have left its secret storage area—the heart of the Vatican, in other words.

Notably, additional reports generated during the same timeframe by elements of the U.S. Intelligence community suggested that Bigelow's information was right on the money, so to speak, and that a massive 200 million Swiss francs was secretly delivered to the Institute for Works of Religion—the Vatican Bank, as it is generally known. To this day, not surprisingly, both the bank and Vatican officials deny any knowledge of such a controversial transfer of funds essentially done on the orders of Adolf Hitler. Seven decades after Hitler and his cronies were defeated much of this saga is still engulfed in a muddy haze of secrecy. Yet, the allegation that somewhere, deep inside the secret vaults and tunnels of the Vatican, there exists a repository for Nazi-purloined treasures just will not go away.

Hungary's crown

The Holy Crown of Hungary, also known as the Crown of Saint Stephen, has a similarly remarkable history, to say the least. Believed to have been fashioned in the 1100s, it has been stolen and recovered on countless occasions, such as when Lajos Kossuth, the Regent-President

The priceless Crown of St. Stephen.

of Hungary, fled the country with it after the collapse of the Hungarian revolution of 1848 and then buried it in a forested area in Transylvania. By 1853, the crown had been successfully recovered and was returned to Buda Castle, Budapest, from where Kossuth had originally pilfered it. But the adventures of the crown were far from over: it was eventually destined to travel overseas.

As the Second World War came to a crashing end for Hitler and Co., and as the Russians were publicly demonstrating their strength all across Hungary, the crown was secretly handed over to the U.S. Army's 86th Infantry Division to ensure that it stayed out of the hands of the Kremlin. A secure, heavily guarded location was chosen to house the priceless, legendary item: none other than the United States Bullion Depository in Kentucky, commonly known as Fort Knox, which holds approximately 2.5 percent of all the gold known to have been refined throughout human history. The crown remained there until January 6, 1978, when it was returned to the people of Hungary, with much fanfare and gratitude given to the United States and President Jimmy Carter for ensuring that the Soviets never succeeded in getting their hands on the legendary crown.

This would be just another story of political intrigue, were it not for one very strange, and previously secret fact: According to a collection of State Department memoranda of 1956 and 1957, at one point in the 1950s, as a means to ensure that the true nature of what they were guarding remained a murky secret, the soldiers at Fort Knox were first told that the crate containing the crown held the wings and engine of a flying saucer! They were later advised that its contents were actually recovered German artwork, gold, and other items of priceless historical value.

C - 5

THE LITTLE MEN OF HANGAR 18

ON MARCH 28, 1975, THE LATE BARRY Goldwater—who served as a major-general in the Air Force, a senator for Arizona, the Republican party's nominee for president in the 1964 election, and the chairman of the U.S. government's Senate Intelligence Committee—wrote the following words to a UFO researcher named Shlomo Arnon: "The subject of UFOs is one that has interested me for some long time. About 10 or 12 years ago I made an effort to find out what was in the building at Wright-Patterson Air Force Base where the information is stored that has been collected by the Air Force, and I was understandably denied this request. It is still classified above Top Secret."[1]

Well, it's certainly not every day you receive a letter like *that* in the mail—and from a U.S. senator and a presidential candidate no less. The building to which Goldwater was referring is allegedly a super-secret location that many UFO researchers believe houses the remnants of one or more crashed UFOs, along with the cryogenically preserved remains of their deceased alien crewmembers. Its memorable moniker is Hangar 18.

Whether it really is a literal hangar or a myriad of underground chambers and tunnels still remains to be seen. That it exists at Wright-Patterson in some fashion, however, is—according to many retired military and intelligence personnel, at least—not a matter of any doubt. Yet the Air Force vehemently disagrees. For its members (publicly, at least), Hangar 18 is no more than a tiresome albatross forever hanging around the military's collective neck. Oh, how they want to strangle that bothersome bird.

Staff at the base categorically (and at times wearily) deny that alien bodies and extraterrestrial spacecraft are secretly held at Wright-Patterson. The terse, official word from the Public Affairs office at Wright-Patterson today, to anyone who dares ask them, is as follows: "Periodically, it is erroneously stated that the remains of extraterrestrial visitors are or have been stored at Wright-Patterson AFB. There are not now nor ever have been, any extraterrestrial visitors or equipment on Wright-Patterson Air Force Base."[2] The Air Force's statement is polite and to the point...one suspects they are constantly itching to scream something along the lines of, "Take that, ufologists, and stick it where the sun don't shine!" Nonetheless, Wright-Patterson has a longstanding and undeniable link to the whole UFO kit and caboodle.

In 1947, General Nathan Twining, who was then the Chief of the Air Materiel Command at the base, initiated the creation of Project Sign, an official operation designed to investigate the burgeoning mystery of UFOs. Sign was shortly thereafter replaced by Project Grudge, which continued to operate from Wright-Patterson. In 1952, Project Blue Book took over the reins from Grudge, before finally closing its pages in 1969. Officially, no evidence was ever found by Sign, Grudge, or Blue Book staff that UFOs were anything more than hoaxes, the results of psychological aberrations, or misidentifications of either natural phenomena or conventional aerial vehicles such as aircraft, balloons, rockets, and satellites. Again, a black eye on the face of ufology—or maybe an outrageous attempt to hide a startling truth of non-terrestrial proportions.

Does the U.S. government have a secret storage area, something like this hangar, for alien bodies?

stringfield's research

One of the most persistent sleuths who have attempted to force open the impenetrable doors of Hangar 18
is Leonard Stringfield. Having served within the shadowy world of intelligence-gathering and analysis during
the Second World War, Stringfield was a prime character to pursue the convoluted mysteries of Hangar 18.
Stringfield had deeply investigated the UFO conundrum
since the early 1950s; it was not until the latter part of the
1970s, however, that he began to almost exclusively focus
his research upon Hangar 18, which he did with success
up until the time of his death in late 1994.

Of the multitude of accounts that reached Stringfield,
one truly fascinating tale came via a dedicated UFO investigator named Charles Wilhelm. It went like this: In
1959, Wilhelm, who was a youngster at the time, was
hired by an elderly lady living in Price Hill, Cincinnati,
to do yard work at her home. Throughout the course
of their various conversations, the issue of UFOs occasionally came up, and the pair mused upon the matter
and what its impact might be if one day revealed to an
unsuspecting populace. When the woman developed ter-
minal cancer, and with her life hanging in the balance,
she elected to confide in Wilhelm a remarkable story of
jaw-dropping proportions.

As Wilhelm listened, enthralled, the woman revealed
how, while serving with the U.S. Air Force at Wright-
Patterson in the early 1950s, she held a Top Secret clearance, and on one occasion had seen two flying saucers that
were held at the base in what she described as a secret hangar. One such craft, she recalled, was in very good shape,

whereas the other showed clear structural signs of having been involved in a serious accident or crash. Wilhelm's informant quietly told him of her personal knowledge of the preserved remains of two nonhuman creatures held at the base. She even had occasion to view the autopsy reports on the entities, Wilhelm told an excited Stringfield. The woman's final words on the matter, which succinctly explained the reasons behind her brave decision to take Wilhelm into her confidence: "Uncle Sam can't do anything to me after I'm in the grave." Right on, lady.

If Wright-Patterson is indeed home to such astonishing alien evidence, from where and when did it originate? Many suggest the answer is the ufological granddaddy of all granddaddies: Roswell, New Mexico, in the summer of 1947.[3]

Roswell

It was the first week of July 1947 when something strange crashed on ranch land in a remote part of Lincoln County, New Mexico—approximately a 90-minute drive from the town of Roswell—and got the military into a state of total turmoil. The incident has since captured the collective imagination of the general public and the media, has been the topic of more than 20 books, has led to investigations undertaken by both the General Accounting Office and a grumbling U.S. Air Force, and, finally, has ensured Roswell and its people a place on the map and a regular influx of tourists eager to get the scoop on everything extraterrestrial.

The undeniably strange event has provoked an avalanche of explanations from those who have valiantly sought—but ultimately failed—to conclusively resolve the matter. Here are a few:

- ⃠ A weather balloon.
- ⃠ A more cumbersome balloon array designed to secretly monitor for early Soviet atomic-bomb tests.
- ⃠ A balloon-based high-altitude-exposure experiment utilizing human guinea pigs.
- ⃠ The crash of a captured German rocket with small monkeys onboard.

Beyond a doubt, the one explanation that, more than any other, just refuses to go away is the theory that a spacecraft from another world crashed in the wilds of Lincoln County, in the process killing its strange crew and accidentally revealing to the U.S. military that we are not alone in the universe. Much of the available data and testimony suggests it was to Wright-Patterson in Ohio that the Roswell debris and dead entities—whatever they might have been—were secretly transferred.

Norman Richards, who served with the 25th Tropic Lightning Division of the U.S. Army, had his own Roswell story to tell. In the summer of 1950, he and a number of other personnel were flown to Lowry Air Force Base in Colorado for a month and a half of training. One day, while on base at Lowry, Richards' group attended a lecture—from a colonel who just happened to be stationed at Wright-Patterson—on the subject of new, experimental aircraft. During the course of the lecture, the controversy surrounding UFOs surfaced. One of the attendees wanted to know if UFOs exist. Richards recalled that the colonel got very excited and told the group they had better believe UFOs exist. Alien bodies, along with wreckage from one of their ships, said the remarkably talkative colonel, had been found and secretly retrieved. The colonel, said Richards, told the group that the recovered materials were under investigation at a secure locale on Wright-Patterson after having been covertly flown in from Roswell.

Similarly, the late Brigadier General Arthur E. Exon—who held the position of commanding officer at Wright-Patterson—confirmed that alien bodies, and the remains of their ship, were secretly transferred to the base after their recovery in Lincoln County, New Mexico, in the summer of 1947. If anyone should know, it would surely be the base's commanding officer, right?

Wright-Patterson

As Stringfield's research into crashed UFOs and Hangar 18 continued, he secured the testimony of further sources who maintained that a secret, off-limits hangar or vault existed somewhere at Wright-Patterson, where the prized alien evidence could be found if one only knew where to look. One such source was a retired major who advised Stringfield—on the condition that his true identity never be revealed to anyone—that in 1952 he had attended a Top Secret briefing at Wright-Patterson on the UFO issue, after which he was given access to a hidden, underground chamber at the base where a number of extraterrestrial corpses were cryogenically preserved. The bodies, Stringfield's Deep Throat told him, were gray-skinned, approximately 4 feet in height, and had large heads.

Wright-Patterson Air Force Base, Ohio:
the rumored home of Hangar 18.

There was an even more amazing (many might say outrageous) story to come. And if Stringfield wasn't the victim of some bizarre practical joke, cruel prank, or officially orchestrated leg-pull to try and demolish the credibility of his quickly expanding dossier of data, it's a tale that takes the saga of Hangar 18 to a completely different level of cosmic controversy. If the story is true, it's not just *dead* aliens that are held at Wright-Patterson; *live* ones are running (or shuffling) around too!

It was a weekend in 1965 when Stringfield's informant, dubbed only "R.M.," chose to visit the National Museum of the United States Air Force—formerly the

United States Air Force Museum—located on the grounds of Wright-Patterson. While his wife was busy studying a captured Nazi V-2 rocket, R.M. wandered off, soon became lost amid the maze of corridors, and finally found himself confronted by a pair of doors adorned with two, large, ominous words: *Off Limits*. Faced with such a sign, I suspect very few of us would be able to resist the temptation to take a peek at what might be on the other side.

Indeed, the sign did not deter R.M. in the slightest, and he tentatively pushed the doors open. On the other side was a room containing a small, large-eyed, heavy-browed creature, clearly unlike any terrestrial life-form, that, in a somewhat comical fashion, shuffled towards R.M. and pointed one of its fingers directly at him. Unsurprisingly, all R.M. could do was stare, utterly dumbstruck, at the alien entity. Suddenly, alarms began going off all throughout the facility, and R.M., fearful that he might soon find himself being grilled by menacing, cigar-chomping generals, high-tailed it out of the room. He finally found his shaky way back to his wife, while military police proceeded to quickly usher everyone out of the building. The alien who gave R.M. the finger, so to speak, apparently elected not to follow and was not seen again.

R.M. told Stringfield that, in his opinion, the alarm was raised because the presumed alien creature had broken free of its confines on the base and was now on the loose, no doubt trying to make good its escape. Notably, R.M. later learned from a retired Air Force colonel that *two* living alien creatures were held at Wright-Patterson in the 1960s, military scientists having, supposedly, successfully created a suitable atmosphere in which to house the interplanetary pair.

As for Stringfield, although he conceded that R.M.'s story was an undeniably fantastic one, he added that, "The Wright-Patterson complex is vast and so are its underground facilities. It is conceivable, if truly live aliens exist, that one may have slipped by the guards into the passageways and surfaced in an upper chamber of the museum."[4] A crazy tale, no doubt, but for Stringfield, nothing was ever too over-the-top when it came to Hangar 18, hence why he chose not to quietly file the story in his gray basket, but instead championed it widely.

As the 1960s became the 1970s, the tales of Hangar 18 continued to proliferate and circulate.

sensitive Activities

Victor Marchetti, a former executive assistant to the deputy director and special assistant to the executive director of the CIA, went on record in the late 1970s that while he was serving with the CIA, UFO-related reports were filed under the heading of what he termed very sensitive activities. Far more significantly, Marchetti admitted that, from time to time, and via high-level sources and colleagues within the CIA, he was privy to accounts relative to alien bodies and at least one crashed UFO, held by Wright-Patterson's Foreign Technology Division. Marchetti's story is far less sensational than that of R.M., but it's made far more important due to Marchetti's prestigious—and provable—background. As was precisely the case with Senator Barry Goldwater, Marchetti was most certainly no tinfoil-hat-wearing wacko.

Hacking into Hangar 18

On October 27, 1992, *Dateline NBC* devoted a segment of its show to the subject of computer hacking, and chose to include certain Q&As with a number of self-confessed hackers. With one of the hackers talking about his ability to easily break into government and military computer systems, NBC flashed across the screen a variety of documentation that had supposedly been obtained by the hacker from Wright-Patterson's computer system. In part it stated, "WRIGHT-PATTERSON AFB/ Catalogued UFO parts list, an underground facility of Foreign...."

At that point, to the disappointment of everyone watching, the camera flashed away and the rest of the document was not shown; however, it was later revealed that at least part of the material downloaded by the hacker was said to reference Top Secret alien-autopsy data stored on Wright-Patterson's computer systems. That's right: to the utter joy of UFO hunters everywhere, Hangar 18 was not dead.

In 1993, *Dateline NBC* broke its silence on this controversial issue, and Susan Adams, who had been the producer of that particular segment of the program, expressed considerable amazement at the incredible response that NBC had received following the airing of the episode.

Hang on a minute. Let's see if we have that right: NBC broadcasts—on primetime television, no less— imagery of secret UFO files and data on alien-autopsies, obtained under circumstances that were wholly illegal, from Wright-Patterson's secret computer banks, and Adams is amazed by the response? What, pray tell, did

Adams and her bosses expect? The production team should have considered itself extremely lucky that the notorious Men in Black of UFO lore did not come knocking—or perhaps banging hard—on the doors of NBC.

Adams continued that the hacker desired to remain anonymous, primarily because his material had allegedly been acquired under circumstances that were hardly lawful, via delving into classified American governmental and military computerized files and archives. Hell yes, he wanted to remain anonymous! One can scarcely begin to imagine what fate—or Air Force security personnel—would have had in store for the unknown hacker if he had been chased down and caught. It wouldn't have been good, that's for sure.

On the matter of the precious data, Adams state that NBC's lawyers had scrutinized it to the finest degree possible, and had become convinced of the complete legitimacy of the acquired, alien-themed material. Moreover, Adams explained that, as the hacker was technically committing a felony, there was absolutely no way that his identity could ever be revealed. Surprising no one who had followed this story, Adams added that although the hacker was acutely aware of the interest his apparent UFO data had provoked, he did not wish to respond in any way.

Matthew Bevan

Matthew Bevan is a self-confessed, and somewhat proud, computer hacker from Wales, United Kingdom, who, as a teenager in the mid-1990s, chose to hack into the gigantic complex of computer systems at Wright-Patterson in search of data on Hangar 18, crashed UFOs, and dead aliens. Bevan, whose story sounds like it strode right out of the 1983 movie *Wargames*, had an interest in computers as far back as the age of 11, when his parents bought him a ZX81 (which is of course now considered a dinosaur) for his birthday, which he eventually traded in for a Commodore Amiga 1200—the computer Bevan was using when he hacked Wright-Patterson in 1994 and 1995.

Wright-Patterson, said Bevan, was an *extremely* simple computer system to get into, and he relished the opportunity to briefly rummage around classified e-mails, Top Secret work files, and Eyes Only documentation on futuristic aircraft. Bevan's teenage naiveté actually led him to confidently believe he had successfully penetrated the secrets of Wright-Patterson without detection by U.S. authorities. Come on! He hacks the Air Force and they don't even get wind of it? Sadly for Bevan, *of course* the Air Force got wind of it. They became extremely irate in the process, and soon contacted British authorities.

It wasn't long before the boy wonder was arrested by Scotland Yard's Computer Crimes Unit (CCU) and charged with hacking Wright-Patterson, NASA, Lockheed, and a variety of additional entities within, or with ties to, the U.S. government. *Deep shit* didn't even begin to describe the position in which Bevan found himself. Notably, at one point while being questioned by personnel about his actions, a Detective-Sergeant Simon Janes, of the CCU, asked Bevan what the term *Hangar 18* meant to him. Bevan—for whom much of this episode merely seemed like an exciting episode of *The

X-Files—replied enthusiastically that it was a storage area for extraterrestrial craft and dead aliens.

Throughout the interview, Scotland Yard's finest kept coming back to Hangar 18, and pummeling him with questions like, Did he view anything unusual on the Wright-Patterson computers? What was his motivation? Bevan nonchalantly told them he was hot on the trail of the U.S. government's most guarded UFO secrets, and nothing more. A few months later, a hearing at Bow Street Magistrates Court in London went ahead; Bevan was out on bail at the time. To add to his problems, the American authorities were now claiming that certain things on the computers he had supposedly hacked into had been changed, perhaps maliciously. Cripes.

Having the audacity to hack the U.S. Air Force in search of alien secrets was one thing. Deliberately altering entire computer systems and creating major headaches for the military, said the U.S. government, was beyond the pale. Uncle Sam wanted swift justice. Bevan's lawyer swung into action and asked to see the evidence demonstrating that Bevan had altered the computer systems. Amazingly, the U.S. military flatly refused to provide any form of evidence, and insisted that the judge just take them at their word. He was not impressed.

It was during this hearing that a U.S. Intelligence operative named Jim Hanson took the stand and said that he was there to represent the U.S. government's interests in the Bevan affair. Bevan's defense continued to push for information to back up the claims of the American government that he had somehow altered their systems, but Hanson would not budge.

As the hearing continued, the prosecution asked Hanson what the American government thought about Bevan's motives regarding his hacking of Wright-Patterson. Hanson admitted that, although Bevan's actions were illegal, no one within officialdom was of the opinion that Bevan was after anything more than UFO data. In other words, Bevan wasn't considered by the Americans to be a secret spy in the employ of the Russians, the Chinese, or the North Koreans, or as someone using his UFO research as a cover for far more nefarious snooping.

Ultimately, Bevan proved to be an extremely lucky young man: U.S. authorities continued to refuse to reveal any evidence relative to the computerized files that he reportedly accessed and supposedly altered—possibly due to legitimate fears that such action might open up even more tricky questions relative to the Hangar 18 controversy. This lack of evidence allowed Bevan to walk free in November 1997.

Today, a naïve teenager no more, Bevan's illegal hacking days are long behind him. But U.S. officialdom has certainly not forgotten its failed attempt to teach him a lesson, the likes of which he would surely never, ever have forgotten. Off the record, officialdom has quietly made it clear to Bevan that, should he contemplate making a trip to the United States, he would be very wise to think again. Accidents can, and do, happen, after all...especially when they're not really accidents.

P.O.W. Art

Irena Scott, a UFO researcher with a special interest in the stories of extraterrestrial bodies secretly held at

Wright-Patterson, has reported on another facet of the controversy. Could the story of Hangar 18 get any more convoluted? Yes, it could. Scott's is an intriguing addition to the story that takes us back to the heart of the Second World War—but it has absolutely *nada* to do with aliens. From 1943 through 1946, a particular section of the base served as a prisoner-of-war camp for several hundred German troops who had been captured during hostilities in both North Africa and Italy.

Scott discovered that on a particular stretch of wall approximately 70 feet long by 20 feet high in the prisoners' mess hall, the captured soldiers had passed their time by painting huge murals that depicted mythological figures from German folklore. Monstrous and gargoyle-like in nature, their green-color, Scott suggested, might very well have provoked rumors pertaining to the remains of little green men housed at Wright-Patterson. It's as good a theory as any, some might say, but it's highly unlikely to satisfy those who see the real story as being far more sensational than a bit of old artwork done by a few bored prisoners-of-war nearly 70 years ago. The curious legend of Wright-Patterson's Hangar 18 and its attendant little men from the stars, it seems, is destined to live on.

c - 6

LONDON'S TUNNELS OF TERROR

ENGLAND'S FAMOUS LONDON UNDERGROUND railway system serves Greater London and parts of the surrounding counties of Essex, Hertfordshire, and Buckinghamshire. It's also the world's oldest underground network of its type: services began on January 10, 1863 on the Metropolitan Railway. Whereas the overall Underground itself is not, of course, a secret location, it certainly has concealed more than its fair share of off-limits sections throughout the course of its long and literally winding existence. Nor is it exactly a stranger to matters of official government secrecy.

Within the dark tunnels of the London
Underground, something monstrous lurks...

At the height of the Second World War, when the
Nazis were engaged in widespread bombing missions on
London, the deep tunnels of the Underground were used
as safe havens for the populace of England's bomb-scarred
capital. Also, during this same time frame, a part of the
Central Line was clandestinely converted into an aircraft
factory, while the Brompton Road Station was massively
reconditioned to become a secret anti-aircraft control center. And, for a while, none other than the British Prime
Minister of the day, Sir Winston Churchill, used the de-
funct Down Street Station as a secret haven from which
to carefully plot retaliation against the swarming forces

of Adolf Hitler. Today, the London Underground has no less than 268 stations and approximately 250 miles of track, making it the longest subsurface railway in the entire world. In addition, by 2007, more than 1 billion passengers were recorded as having used the Underground since its creation.

According to some, however, the London Underground is home to much more than just trains, tracks, and countless commuters; deep within this subsurface maze of dark and old tunnels, strange and terrible things are said to lurk. And the British government, not exactly in control of the darkness that is spreading uncontrollably beneath the ancient capital city, is determined to keep the truth of these terrifying underground secrets steadfastly away from the eyes and ears of the public and the media.

Tales of strange creatures, ghosts, and monsters roaming the sinister depths of the London Underground have proliferated for years. In fictional format, they were most famously portrayed in the 1981 movie *An American Werewolf in London*, in which the hairy wolfman of the movie's title preyed on an unfortunate late-night traveler. And in *Reign of Fire*, a 2002 movie starring Matthew McConaughey and Christian Bale, fire-breathing dragons surfaced from the old tunnels and subsequently laid waste to first the British Isles and ultimately the rest of the planet.

'Death Line'

Some of the older stories of monstrous entities prowling the dark tunnels under Britain's capital city were incorporated into a 1972 movie called *Death Line*, starring horror-movie regulars Christopher Lee (*Dracula*) and Donald Pleasance (*Halloween*). The entertaining movie tells the story of a collapse, in the latter part of the 19th century, at a new station that is being constructed at Russell Square. Unfortunately, when the accident happens, a number of Irish workers are presumed killed. The company behind the work goes bankrupt, and no one can afford to dig out the bodies of the dead.

As you might have already deduced, the laborers don't actually starve to death or end up crushed beneath mountains of rock and rubble. Instead, they manage to survive, and they breed deep below the ground. Then, 80 years later, the last few surviving offspring—who dwell deep within the heart of the myriad underground tunnels—do their utmost to replenish their food supply from the platform at Russell Square. "Food supply," of course, equates to passengers. As the publicity blurb that accompanied *Death Line* (or *Raw Meat*, as it was released in the United States) went, "Beneath modern London buried alive in its plague-ridden tunnels lives a tribe of once humans. Neither men nor women, they were less than animals—they are the raw meat of the human race."

underground killings

In reality, not everyone is so certain that the reports of cannibalistic sub-humans rampaging around the old tunnels of the London Underground are merely the stuff of fantasy. In fact, one person said he absolutely *knew* such stories are more than fiction. His story is as unbelievable as it is morbidly engaging. Before his 2007 death,

Frank Wiley, who served in the British Police Force, had an astounding story to tell about his investigations of a number of weird killings in the London Underground, always late at night, in a clearly delineated period of time that covered 1967 to 1969. The killings, Wiley said, occurred in at least three stations, and were hushed up by the police, who claimed the attacks were merely late-night muggings.

On the contrary, Wiley explained, the "muggings" were nothing of the sort. The attacks were far more horrific in nature. There were, he recalled, seven deaths during the time he was assigned to the investigations. He said the modus operandi of the killer was always exactly the same: The bodies of the victims—a couple of whom were commuters, whereas the rest of them were hobos looking for shelter on cold nights—were found, always after at least 10 p.m., a significant distance into the tunnels, with arms and/or legs viciously removed...possibly *gnawed* off. Stomachs were ripped open, innards were torn out, and throats were violently slashed. It was clear that a man-eater—or, worse still, a whole group of man-eaters—was seemingly prowling around the most shadowy corners of London's dark underworld after sunset. It, or they, had only one goal: to seek out fresh flesh with which to nourish their ever-hungry bellies.

Could it have been the case that the killings were the work of a rampaging animal, possibly one that had escaped from a local zoo or a private menagerie and was now on the loose far below the capital city? Or might the deaths have been due to desperate, suicidal people who threw themselves under the speeding trains, after which their remains were violently dragged into the tunnels and under the steel wheels of the racing carriages? Wiley strongly believed these scenarios *not* to be the case.

There was another very good reason why the deaths were not ascribed to wild beasts or suicides: the presence of a terrifying character seen at some point in 1968 by two workmen who were repairing a particular stretch of track on the Bakerloo Line (a 14-mile section of the London Underground that was constructed in 1906). The terrifying character, stated Wiley, was a bearded, wild-haired man, dressed in tattered and filthy clothing. When one of the workers challenged the mysterious figure with a large ratchet, the man came closer, in a weird, faltering, stumbling manner. To the horror of the pair, he held his arms out in front of him, bared a mouth of decayed teeth in their direction, and uttered a low, guttural growl. The strange figure then slowly backed away, eventually turning, and then suddenly running deeper into the tunnel, until he was finally, and forever, lost from view. Unsurprisingly, the workmen elected not to give chase, but instead raced to the nearest station and summoned the police, who questioned the petrified men vigorously. Wiley further added that secret orders quickly came down to the police investigators on the case—from the British Government's Home Office, which focuses on a host of issues relative to national security—to wrap everything up, and quickly.

Wiley maintained that a secret liaison with Home Office personnel revealed that there were unverified rumors of deeper, very ancient, crudely built tunnels—that reportedly dated back centuries; long, long before the advent of trains and railways—existing far below even the Underground. There was even speculation they may have been constructed as far back as the Roman invasion of Britain that began in 43 AD. Precisely who had constructed the older tunnels, and who it was that might have emerged from them to wreak havoc on the Underground in the 1960s, was never revealed to Wiley's small team of personnel. He said, "Probably no one really knew, anyway. Only that someone, like the character seen by the workmen, was coming up from somewhere, killing, taking parts of the bodies, and then they were always gone again."[1] Wiley added, "It all got pushed under the rug when the Home Office said so. And when the last killing I was involved in [occurred], in 1969, I didn't hear much after that; just rumors there might have been more deaths in the 70s upward. I don't know."[2]

Wiley's final words on the grisly affair, in 2004, were, "There's more to the [*Death Line*] film than people know. My thought then, and which it still is today, is someone making the film heard the stories, [and] the deaths we investigated. They had to have: The film was too close to what happened. And I think we didn't have control of the tunnels, and someone up in the government knew. Perhaps it's still going on. That would be a thought."[3]

Indeed, it would be a thought. A very sobering and disturbing thought.

A Dangerous Patient

Perhaps of relevance to the sensational story of Frank Wiley is the equally strange tale of Jonathan Downes, the director of the British-based Center for Fortean Zoology, which is dedicated to the investigation of mysterious animals, such as Bigfoot, the Abominable Snowman, the Chupacabra, and the Loch Ness Monster. Between 1982 and 1985, Downes worked as a nurse at the Royal Counties Hospital, near the English city of Exeter, Devonshire. While employed at the hospital, Downes heard stories of how, at some point in the 1940s—and possibly even on more than one occasion—disturbing things were afoot at the hospital that had a direct link with the tales of strange goings-on beneath the London Underground.

According to one particular doctor with whom Downes had the opportunity to speak in the early 1980s, the events all began with a series of late-night telephone calls to the hospital from the Lord Lieutenant of the County, from the Earl of Devon, and from elements of the Devonshire Police Force—all secretly informing senior personnel at the hospital that a highly dangerous patient was to be brought to the hospital within the hour, who would require special care and handling in an isolated, locked room. The doctor told Downes that around 45 minutes later, a police vehicle arrived at Starcross Hospital, reversed with a screech up to a side door, and then several police officers tumbled out of the back, while simultaneously trying to hang on to what the doctor said resembled a dirt-encrusted and hair-covered caveman.

The man-beast was reportedly young-looking, perhaps in its early 20s, was around 6 feet in height, was completely naked, and had a heavy brow, wide nose, and very muscular arms and legs. For three days, the creature was securely held at the hospital, Downes was advised, before it was transferred to an unspecified, government-run location amid the twists and turns of the London Underground. Its fate remains unknown. That is, unless it escaped from its subterranean confines to live wild amid the mass of tunnels, and survived by dining upon certain unfortunate souls traveling the London Underground by night who just tragically happened to be on the wrong platform at the wrong hour. Maybe one of Frank Wiley's cannibals was actually Jonathan Downes' wild-man.

Ghostly Attack

In some respects, this story eerily parallels that of a man named Colin Campbell, who maintains that while traveling home on the London Underground in the mid-1960s, he had a nightmarish encounter with a very similar beast. According to Campbell, it was late at night, and he was the only person to get off the train at its scheduled stop on the Northern Line. As the train pulled away from the unusually deserted platform, and as Campbell made his way towards the exit, he claims to have heard a strange growl coming from behind him. He quickly spun around and was shocked to see a large, hairy, ape-like animal lumbering across the platform towards the track.

Most bizarre of all, however, was the fact that the beast was seemingly spectral in nature, rather than flesh and blood. Indeed, around three-quarters of its body was above the platform, while its legs were curiously transparent, and, incredibly, passed right *through* the platform. Campbell further asserts that as he stood in awe, too shocked to move, the beast continued to walk through the concrete, right onto the tracks, and then straight through the wall directly behind the tunnel. Was it, perhaps, the ghostly form of the hairy wild-man taken from Starcross Hospital all those years earlier? Or was it the spectral version of another such creature, similarly captured years before? Today, decades on, we may never know. But sightings of weird creatures on the London Underground are not solely limited to rampaging man-beasts.

Big cats

For the last 40 years or so, tales have abounded—to the point that they are now at almost ridiculous epidemic levels—of sightings of so-called big cats on the loose throughout pretty much the entire British countryside. Precisely what they are, where they come from, and why no one seems to be able to successfully capture or kill one is a matter of both heated argument and ongoing debate. Long before the present-day controversy began, however, these elusive beasts may very well have called the London Underground their home.

One witness, Maureen Abbott, a woman in her late 20s, saw what she describes as a large black panther racing along the track as she stood, alone, awaiting a train on the Bakerloo Line late one winter evening in either 1954 or 1955. Describing the animal as running very fast, she said that as it passed her, it quickly looked in her direction, with a menacing frown on its visage, before vanishing into the darkness of the tunnels. Although Abbott did not see the creature again, she has never forgotten her brief, terrifying encounter with the unknown, deep beneath the city of London.

Two days later, Abbott was visited at her home by a government official who advised her in relaxed tones, while they sat and drank cups of tea, not to talk about the experience. Of course, this aspect of Abbott's story inevitably conjures up Men in Black imagery. If true, it suggests that elements of the British government may wish to keep quiet the fact that wild animals are on the loose in the heart of London's old tunnels.

British Museum Station

Physical creatures aside, encounters of a distinctly spectral nature have also been reported in the London Underground for decades—on countless occasions and in numerous tunnels. They have also been the subjects of official secrecy sanctions.

For many years prior to British Museum Station's closure on September 25, 1933, a local myth circulated to the effect that the ghost of an ancient Egyptian haunted the station. Dressed in a loincloth and headdress, the figure would emerge late at night into the labyrinth of old tunnels. In fact, the rumor grew so strong that a London newspaper even offered a significant monetary reward to anyone who was willing to spend the night there. Somewhat surprisingly, not a single, solitary soul took the newspaper up on its generous offer.

The story took a far stranger turn after the station was shut down, however. The comedy-thriller movie, *Bulldog Jack*, which was released in 1935, included in its story a secret tunnel that ran from British Museum Station to the Egyptian Room at the British Museum. The station in the film is a wholly fictional one dubbed Bloomsbury, but the scenario presented in the film was based upon the enduring legend of the ghost of British Museum Station.

Oddly enough, on the exact same night that the movie was released in British cinemas, two women disappeared from the platform at Holborn—the next station along the line from the British Museum. Strange marks were later found on the walls of the closed station at the British Museum, and more sightings of the ghost were reported, along with weird moaning noises heard coming from behind the walls of the tunnels. Not surprisingly, tales began to quickly circulate that the police had uncovered some dark and terrible secret about a paranormal killer on the tracks that had to be kept hidden from the populace at all costs. In other words, this was a strange, yet eerily similar precursor to the 1960s recollections of Frank Wiley.

London Underground officials were, for a significant period of time, forced to dismiss the story, and there has always been an outright denial of the existence of any secret tunnel extending from British Museum Station to the museum's Egyptian Room. Nevertheless, the story was resurrected in Keith Lowe's 2001 novel, *Tunnel Vision*, in which the lead character states, while trying to impress and scare his girlfriend at the same time, "If you listen carefully when you're standing at the platform at Holborn, sometimes—just sometimes—you can hear the wailing of Egyptian voices floating down the tunnel toward you."[4]

British Museum Station is also said to be home to a ghostly figure that roams the tunnels dressed in a large coat, tall hat, and gloves. Supposedly, the ghost is that of one William Terriss, an actor who was stabbed to death near the Adelphi Theater in December 1897.

Bank Station

And then there is the ghost of Bank Station: During the construction of Bank Station, workmen are said to have awakened the spirit of a woman named Sarah, better known as the Black Nun, whose brother, Philip, was said to be a bank employee executed for forgery, and who worked close to the station. According to legend, Sarah's spectral form still roams the platforms and tunnels, looking for her long-gone brother.

ufo storage

UFOs play a role in the London Underground controversy too. In fact, the imagery suggests the existence of nothing less than a full-blown Hangar 18–style facility somewhere under London. A persistent story that absolutely refuses to die asserts that in 1944 or 1945 a detachment of the British 8th Army found a semi-intact UFO and its crew on moorland on the English-Scottish border. Knowledgeable and respected sources maintain that details of the case reached key sources within the military infrastructure of the day. To fully ascertain the facts, we need to go back to 1955 and a news report put out at the time by a certain American journalist, Dorothy Kilgallen (who happened to be the last journalist to interview Jack Ruby, the man who shot and killed Lee Harvey Oswald in Dallas, Texas, in November 1963): "British scientists and airmen, after examining the wreckage of one mysterious flying ship, are convinced these strange aerial objects are not optical illusions or Soviet inventions, but are flying saucers which originate on another planet. The source of my information is a British official of Cabinet rank who prefers to remain unidentified. 'We believe on the basis of our inquiry thus far, that the saucers were staffed by small men—probably under four feet tall. It's frightening, but there is no denying the flying saucers come from another planet.'"[5]

A similar account comes via Stan Beech, whose father served in an office of the Royal Air Force during the latter stages of the Second World War. According to Beech, his father was involved, during 1944 and 1945, in the analysis of aerial photographs taken by Royal Air Force pilots of Nazi airfields, ammunition storage areas, and factories. On one specific occasion, however, while liaising with senior figures in the operation, he was exposed to a number of ground-based photographs displaying the crash of a wedge-shaped object on a hillside somewhere in the north of England during the early 1940s. Beech further elaborated that sprawled around the strange craft were several small bodies with large, bald heads, and dressed in gray, one-piece flying suits.

By Beech's own admission, his father was never told from where, exactly, the vehicle and its strange crew originated, nor did he know what—if indeed *any*—conclusions were reached by those tasked with carefully examining the evidence. Beech's father was informed, however, that the object was considered by British authorities to be a matter of extreme concern, and that all of the material—the bodies, the craft, and the photographs—still existed in a sealed chamber somewhere in a series of secret rooms in the London Underground.

🚫

With stories of hairy man-beasts, dead aliens and crashed UFOs, animalistic cannibals, mysterious big cats, and a dizzying assortment of specters prowling around the depths of the London Underground (and not forgetting, of course, all the governmental secrecy and concern about these particularly problematic matters), we might very well legitimately ask: *What else* lurks within the underground shadows of Britain's capital city? Perhaps in time, those mysterious tunnels—and the government that has carefully monitored them for so long—will finally elect to give up all their bizarre and disturbing secrets. Until then, however, if, late one night, you ever find yourself all alone in the London Underground, take careful heed: *They*—in all of their varied and hideous forms—may be watching you, just waiting for the right opportunity to pounce and prey...

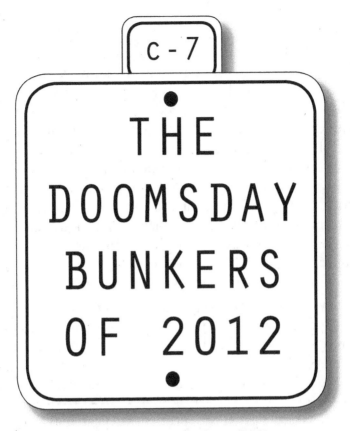

C - 7

THE DOOMSDAY BUNKERS OF 2012

MOST PEOPLE WILL RECALL THAT WHEN THE tragic events of September 11, 2001, occurred, the vice president, Richard "Dick" Cheney, was secretly whisked away to what has famously become known as an undisclosed location. Since that fateful day, the world's media has spent a significant amount of time and effort trying to identify the secret locale to which Cheney and his posse quickly fled. There is certainly no shortage of notable candidates.

In May 2009, while attending the Gridiron Club dinner in Washington D.C., the vice president, Joe Biden, committed the ultimate cardinal sin—in the eyes of Cheney, Dubya, and Condoleezza, no doubt—when he openly revealed to those present his knowledge of a secret underground bunker housed beneath the old U.S. Naval Observatory, which, today, is the home of the vice president himself. As the story goes, upon getting the gig as V.P., Biden was given a tour of the entire facility by a young naval officer. This tour included the classified, below-ground area, which was protected by a huge steel door. During Biden's tour the very same officer quietly informed him that after Cheney's miraculous vanishing act on 9/11, it was from right within the heart of this sub-surface installation that Cheney's personnel were conducting their damage assessment of the terror attacks.

When this particular story about Biden's apparent spectacular slip of the tongue surfaced in the mainstream media, White House staffers—or, more correctly, damage-control experts—were quick to deny its validity. Presidential spin-doctors earnestly announced, practically

The U.S. Naval Observatory. Accounts suggest this is where V.P. Cheney was secretly taken on 9/11.

bellowing, to all those willing to listen, that the whole thing was a big mistake. Honestly, it really was! What Biden was *actually* talking about was not a secret underground world at all, but merely an upstairs room in the building from where the regular, day-to-day work of the vice president is routinely undertaken. The story was a *non*-story, and those were the final words of the Oval Office. Not everyone, however, was buying the government's attempts to smooth things over. In fact, unfortunately for Biden and the new Prez, who had quite enough on his plate already, practically *no one* was buying it.

During the latter months of 2002, for example, locals living in the area of the Observatory were plagued and annoyed, both day and night, by the rumbling sounds of extensive underground construction in their direct vicinity. Those same locals were duly sent letters from the superintendent of the installation informing them of

The home of the U.S. vice president.

the reportedly sensitive and classified nature of the construction program. Not only that, but the completion of the project, at the absolute earliest opportunity, was deemed to be both vital and a matter of national security. Of course, openly telling people something like that is a guarantee that gossip will spread like wild-fire all across those pleasant, white picket fences—and it most surely did spread. Maybe people, it seems, should have listened more closely to Biden's words, rather than to those of White House aides. The Naval Observatory is not the only site that has been suggested as Cheney's private hideaway, however.

Fingers have also been pointed at the Alternate Joint Communications Center, located within Raven Rock Mountain, Pennsylvania, only seven miles from Camp David, the presidential country retreat. Constructed in the early years of the 1950s, the installation—also referred to as Raven Rock and as Site-R—is designed to allow for at least *some* form of continuation of government in the event of a nuclear strike upon the nation's capital. Whether Raven Rock itself can withstand a direct strike, however, is unknown. Nevertheless, the location is reported to be impressive and futuristic. Buried deeply within the mountain, it can comfortably house at least 3,000 people for a considerable period of time, overflowing, as it apparently is, with an abundance of food, fresh water, and clean air. Not bad, provided you happen to be on the *inside*, rather than the *outside*, when the gigantic mushroom clouds start blossoming. It is the perfect place for Vice President Cheney to have been secretly transferred.

On May 25, 2007, the Federal Register (the official journal of the government) stated in a Department of Defense policy document that dealt directly with Raven Rock Mountain, titled "Conduct on the Pentagon Reservation": "The use of cameras or other visual recording devices on the Pentagon Reservation is prohibited.... It shall be unlawful to make any photograph, sketch, picture, drawing, map, or graphical representation of the Pentagon Reservation without first obtaining permission of the Pentagon Force Protection Agency, Installation Commander, or the Office of the Assistant to the Secretary of Defense for Public Affairs."[1]

In non-bureaucratic terms, this means unless you have some weird masochistic desire to incur the wrath of just about every agency of the government that can ruin your day then stay the hell away from Raven Rock.

The 2012 Phenomena

There is a far more disturbing aspect to the story of secret underground installations constructed, or still undergoing construction, to house government officials in the event of a national emergency.

For a number of years, dark rumors have circulated that government agencies all around the world are secretly working to build or revamp huge underground realms to house senior, elite elements of the establishment who are aware that a worldwide, planetary upheaval will cause massive devastation on December 21, 2012, as many assert was predicted centuries ago by the Maya. Sounds too bizarre to be true? Or might those paranoid souls actually be correct? Let's take a look at what we know, what we think we know, and what *they* may not be telling us, or preparing us for.

A great deal of what is spoken about, written about, and lectured on, when it comes the 2012 phenomenon, is, frankly, arrant nonsense that merely plays up to the worst fears and anxieties of the gullible, the wide-eyed, and the under-informed. Many of those fears and anxieties stem from deep misunderstandings about what, exactly, the Maya said, or did *not* say, 2,000 years ago. Plus, there is no doubt that with our civilization filled to bursting with tsunamis, earthquakes, terrorist attacks, Middle Eastern conflicts, avian flu, catastrophic oil leaks, drastic changes in weather, and melting ice caps, many people really *do* see the final days approaching.

Hollywood has hardly helped matters either. Blockbuster movies such as *Children of Men*, *28 Days Later*, *I am Legend*, *Knowing*, *Dawn of the Dead*, and, of course, *2012*, are great fun to watch, but they have all given end-of-the-world scenarios a lot of publicity, and mountains of depressing food for thought throughout the course of the last decade or so. And in the process, those movies have helped nurture apocalypse-driven belief systems that the end might be right around the corner. But is it?

The Mayas were a curious bunch, to be sure; and the means by which a determination has been made that something dramatic—for good, bad, or somewhere in between—may occur on December 21, 2012, is an extremely complex one. It all stems from something called the Mayan Long Count Calendar, which suggests that the end of one particular Earth-cycle will fall on December 21, 2012, some 5,125 years after that cycle commenced.

Many people have come to the conclusion that something dramatic—for good, bad, or somewhere in between—will occur on that date. But a careful, unbiased study of Mayan lore reveals that, in actuality, the notion that the world will literally come to a horrific end, or that civilization will come crashing down around us on that day is very murky and difficult to fathom. For example, precisely *nowhere* in the Mayan legends are there any references to the sky falling in, the oceans overwhelming the land, or rolling firestorms overtaking the planet. In other words, the end of a cycle does not necessarily mean the end of all things. Rather, it's the way in which that potentially emotive word, *cycle*, has been used that leaves its meaning so open to interpretation.

The Mayas believed that life on Earth progressed in cycles. Today, we are said to be living in the fourth cycle; the previous ones were, supposedly, failed attempts by the gods to create the perfect environment on our little world. But what comes next, in the fifth cycle, said to begin after December 12, 2012? Well, that's the big question to which we are all eagerly awaiting the answer. (Some of us are, anyway.)

For some 2012 students, that doomsday date may mark the return of Nibiru—or Planet X—a world alleged to be a part of our own solar system, but whose orbit around the sun is so massive that only once in an extraordinarily long period of time does it ever come into view. Some say it's going to do exactly that in December 2012. And guess what: Its orbit is going to bring it so close to the Earth that planet-wide disaster is all but inevitable. Nevermind that such a large planetary body should already be viewable via advanced telescopes if it's already on its lumbering journey towards us. Nevermind that the entire Nibiru hypothesis was utterly unknown prior to 1995, when a woman named Nancy Lieder, who claimed to be in contact with aliens from a distant star-system called Zeta Reticuli was told that the return of Nibiru, and its attendant, powerful gravitational pull, would provoke a massive polar shift on our world that would result in unbridled chaos and death on an unimaginable scale. Nevermind that Lieder originally said the date of the disaster was going to be 2003. Now, we are told, it's going to be 2012. Ho-hum.

Others suggest the end will come via:

- ⊘ The mighty wrath of a theoretical God.
- ⊘ A pulverizing comet.
- ⊘ A planet-swallowing black hole.
- ⊘ A nuclear confrontation in the Middle East that rapidly erupts into planet-wide atomic-warfare.
- ⊘ An unrelenting and incurable virus.
- ⊘ Hostile aliens.

There is also the view that the only thing likely to change is humankind's mindset. In a best-case scenario, we will find ourselves on a new pathway toward world peace, enlightenment, and a renewed respect for our world and each other. Yeah, I know; kind of boring, and hardly the stuff of a big-bucks Hollywood movie. But it *has* been presented as a viable option.

On the other hand, we may all wake up safely on December 22 to find that absolutely nothing has changed in the slightest, and we can look forward to opening our Christmas presents only a few days later without fear of

Armageddon. After all, not a single prophecy in the history of the planet has ever been proven conclusively to have come 100 percent true, so why should the 2012 fears be any different? It's a perfectly reasonable question to ask. Unfortunately, "nothing is going to happen" fails to strike much of a chord with the media, the populace, or the domain of onscreen entertainment. "Worldwide catastrophe is only months away" *does*, however. All of which brings us to a critical issue: the extent to which such End Times beliefs—valid or not so valid—may have even infected the collective mind of the world's governments.

Norway

In 2010, a highly controversial communication allegedly written and circulated by an unnamed Norwegian politician was widely published across the Internet and attracted a flurry of major attention in the process. It has been dismissed by many as nothing more than a tasteless, fear-mongering hoax, which it may very well be. But it contains at least a couple of intriguing nuggets of verifiable truth, which has ensured the controversy remains. It reads as follows:

> I am a Norwegian politician. I would like to say that difficult things will happen from the year 2008 till the year 2012. The Norwegian government is building more and more underground bases and bunkers. When asked, they simply say that it is for the protection of the people of Norway. When I enquire when they are due to be finished, they reply before 2011. Israel is also doing the same and many

other countries too. My proof that what I am saying is true is in the photographs I have sent of myself and all the Prime Ministers and ministers I tend to meet and am acquainted with. They know all of this, but they don't want to alarm the people or create mass panic. Planet X is coming, and Norway has begun with storage of food and seeds in the Svalbard area and in the arctic north with the help of the U.S. and EU [European Union] and all around in Norway. They will only save those who are in the elite of power and those that can build up again: doctors, scientists, and so on. As for me, I already know that I am going to leave before 2012 to go the area of Mosjøen where we have a deep underground military facility. There we are divided into sectors, red, blue and green. The signs of the Norwegian military are already given to them and the camps have already been built a long time ago. The people that are going to be left on the surface and die with along the others [sic] will get no help whatsoever. The plan is that 2,000,000 Norwegians are going to be safe, and the rest will die.[2]

Hoax, joke, a distortion of reality, or an earnest and honest attempt to reveal the shocking truth of a dark fate that awaits us all in a very short time? We would all like to know the answer to that one. One thing is certain, however: The Norwegian government is preparing for the possibility of some sort of future, hypothetical cataclysmic event—not necessarily linked to 2012. It revolves around something called the Svalbard Global

Seed Vault, which is situated on the Norwegian island of Spitzbergen. The SGSV acts as a secure repository for countless plant and crop seeds, partly in the event that some sort of *above*-surface disaster will require a *below*-surface attempt to rejuvenate the Norwegian landscape and populace. Interestingly, within UFO research circles, there have been longstanding rumors of a flying saucer having slammed into the ground on Spitzbergen back in the early 1950s, instantly killing its crew on impact. But I digress...a worldwide disaster just around the corner is far more important than a 60-year-old UFO crash could ever be. (That is, unless you happened to have been one of the unlucky pilots of that UFO.)

As far back as 1984, Norway's Nordic Gene Bank was quietly collecting seeds and storing them within the depths of an old coal mine on Spitzbergen. More than a quarter of a century later, things have been taken to a whole new level—and I *do* mean literally a whole new level: Extending nearly 400 feet into and under a mountain on the island and controlled by what is known as the Nordic Genetic Resource Center, the SGSV is an incredibly impressive setup, which would surely make the builders of Hangar 18 green with envy.

In February 2008, after almost two years of construction, the installation was proudly unveiled, amid the startling revelation that it was *already* home to more than 1.5 million distinct seed types. And with countless safeguards to protect its precious cargo (possibly even for a period of thousands of years), this static, Noah's Ark of plants quickly caught the attention of the world's media—particularly so when it was revealed that numerous countries had a financial stake in its construction and content, including Australia, the United Kingdom, Switzerland, and Sweden. Even the Rockefeller Foundation and Bill Gates provided funding in the millions. Does Bill, perhaps, know something the rest of us don't? Will he be making a quick trip to Spitzbergen around, say, December 18 or 19, 2012? Maybe he'll have the presence of mind to fly in a week or two earlier, just to be safe.

Whatever the truth, the Norwegian government prefers to focus more upon the scientific importance of the project, rather than having to constantly answer awkward, survivalist questions about 2012. The fact is that the SGSV *could*, in an emergency situation, offer some degree of survival for a significant number of people. Providing you're Norwegian. But what if, like most of the world's population, you're not? The word *screwed* might well pop up in the minds of many.

China

China has also been the target of claims in recent years that it has greatly expanded its plans to construct secret installations, either underground or burrowed right out of dense hills, as a result of a forthcoming, prophesied apocalypse. The most visible such place is located on the southernmost tip of Hainan Island, in the South China Sea, and has become known as Sanya Base. Although many Western military analysts believe the facility to be a secret installation designed for the construction, maintenance, and storage of an ever-growing armada of Chinese nuclear submarines, not everyone is certain that's all it is. Vast tunnels more than 60 feet high have been photographed in and around the base and are said to expand into gigantic caverns that run far below the green hills. Maybe this really is merely China's attempt to revamp its submarine fleet via the rapid construction of countless new underwater craft. However, the vast sculpting of Sanya is still underway right now, which has left more than a few 2012 researchers wondering if, time-wise, there might be a connection to the old Mayan predictions.

Russia

Some say Russia, too, is pulling out all the stops to complete the construction of a multitude of underground survival facilities before 2012 hits us, particularly in some of the more remote areas of the land. Two such bases are buried deep within the Yamantau and Kosvinsky Mountains in the Urals. And make no mistake: The installations are very real. Rudimentary construction at both sites was confirmed in the late 1970s by spy satellites of the United States's National Reconnaissance Office (NRO). Today, the bases have progressed significantly, and data recently collected by other U.S. satellites suggests that expansion of both places in the last few years has been widespread and intense. The Kosvinsky site, for example, is now protected by around 1,000 feet of granite. It is a self-contained hub capable, rumor has it, of comfortably housing in excess of 50,000 individuals. As for the Yamantau base...well, one U.S. intelligence source has suggested it is the size of the Washington, D.C. area within the Beltway.

Then there is Kapustin Yar, a secret Russian site established in 1946 in Astrakhan Oblast, between Volgograd and Astrakhan, dedicated to the research, development, and deployment of rocket-based technologies. Rumors coming out of Russia and data collected from NRO spy satellites, points toward continued underground digging and construction at Kapustin Yar. Why? To further advance Russian rocket research? Or to excavate a place to hide out when the storm hits?

Better known as the Russian Area 51, Zhitkur is a highly secret and incredibly well guarded installation built below a seemingly innocuous small town in the region of Volgograd Oblast. In the very same way that rumors and whistleblower testimony suggests that recovered alien spacecraft are being studied and test-flown at Area 51, Nevada, similar tales surround Zhitkur. Stories emanating from former employees of the base tell of top-secret studies of crashed UFOs. Darker accounts reveal that the Russians are hard at work developing deadly super-viruses at Zhitkur that will have the ability to lethally target specific races of people, while leaving others completely free of infection. All of those rumors are overshadowed by accounts similar to those emanating from Kapustin Yar—that extensive tunnel-boring activity is the order of the day at Zhitkur. And time, the unsettling rumors suggest, is rapidly running out.

People once sang, "The Russians are coming! The Russians are coming!" Maybe today it's the Russians' turn to sing another song: "2012 is coming! 2012 is coming!"

With Norway, Russia, and China now dissected, what of the United States?

The United States

Skeptics of the doomsday theories surrounding 2012 suggest that if such a calamity really was imminent, then the United States would by now be fully engaged in such a tremendously large program to construct massive shelters all across the country that it would be nearly impossible to hide them from the populace and the media. Those same skeptics fail to note, however, that—as this book demonstrates—the United States is *already* peppered with an impressive number of large, strengthened, underground domains.

The U.S. government does not need to build more underground outposts to protect the elite in the event the Mayas really did get it right: *They have had them for decades.* Providing a safe haven for government and military officials in the event of a national emergency of apocalyptic proportions is something that has been planned for pretty much ever since the splitting of the atom in the 1940s. Unless the world is faced with an event in 2012 that exceeds even the horrendous destruction that a nuclear war would bring, safe havens like Raven Rock might provide just as much protection from Mayan prophecy as they might from a multi-megaton Chinese nuke.

A variation on the theory that the U.S. government has ample secure underground installations in which its highest echelons are guaranteed some degree of survival when December 21, 2012 strikes suggests that officialdom is also secretly preparing to utilize many of the natural caves and man-made mines that can be found all across the United States as refuges from whatever might occur on that fateful December day. This particular theory provoked a wealth of debate in the online realm of conspiracy theorizing when, on March 26, 2009, the U.S. Fish and Wildlife Service (FWS) issued a widely circulated press release recommending that cavers and members of the public all across the United States should cease and desist from entering deep caves, caverns, and mines. Inevitably, this led to an unsettling rumor that the government was issuing this demand as a means to slowly and subtly commandeer and control such underground havens, and wrest them away from public access before 2012 arrives.

The official version of events was quite different, however. According to the FWS, their reason for requesting that the U.S. populace desist from entering such places was due to a fungal condition severely affecting the North American bat population: White-Nose Syndrome. In the words of the FWS: "The evidence collected to date indicates that human activity in caves and mines may be assisting the spread of WNS. This fungus grows best in the cold and wet conditions common to caves and abandoned mines and likely can be transported inadvertently from site to site on boots and gear of cave visitors. It is generally recommended that cavers avoid all caves and mines containing hibernating bats, even in states where WNS is not known to occur."[3]

The FWS additionally called for a "voluntary moratorium, effective immediately, on all caving activity in states known to have hibernacula affected by WNS," adding that "scientific activities that involve entry into caves or mines where bats reside should be evaluated to determine if the activity has the potential to facilitate the spread of WNS.... These recommendations will remain in effect until the mechanisms behind transmission of WNS are understood, and/or the means to mitigate the risk of human-assisted transport are developed."[4]

Was this an ingenious cover story on the part of the U.S. Fish and Wildlife Service, or is the whole idea just plain batty? Time may ultimately provide the answer. And if the 2012 theories do possess even a modicum of merit, the biggest conspiracy of all may well be contained in the following question: Why aren't huge subsurface facilities—whether natural or man-made—being made ready for the rest of us who do *not* have the luxury of holding prestigious government positions?

An answer, perhaps, might be found by looking at the final scenes of the darkly comic 1964 movie *Dr. Strangelove*: When the U.S. president, his staff, and senior military personnel realize that human civilization is quickly nearing its end, they hastily envisage a plan in which, while everyone else is left to fry in a worldwide, radioactive nightmare, a small band of select governmental individuals will head deep underground, with a plentiful supply of resources, and a significant number of nubile chicks to help repopulate the decimated human race, before one day resurfacing to start all over again. *Dr. Strangelove* is harrowing, nightmarish, and fiction. Let's hope that as December 21, 2012 gets closer and closer, this entire controversy, for which we have the Mayas to thank, proves to be fiction too.

c - 8

THE NIGHTMARE AT DULCE

THE WILD SAGA OF THE NOTORIOUS UNDER-ground base at Dulce, Rio Arriba County, New Mexico, is as fantastic as it is terrifying. It is a tale filled with hard-to-define rumors, outrageous government deceit and disinformation, hostile extraterrestrials from beyond our solar system, and dark secrets of an alien nature emanating from within the black heart of mysterious subterranean caverns. (It is not an exaggeration to say it's a saga that would have been worthy of an entire season of *The X-Files*, nevermind a single episode.) When one carefully peels away the distortions, the myths, and the lies surrounding this base, what remains just might be a nightmarish reality of otherworldly proportions.

A veritable army of evil alien intruders have, for decades, made their home within a vast, futuristic underworld deep below Archuleta Mesa—a huge peak that extends 9,078 feet above sea level in Rio Arriba County. Most ominous of all: the expected warning to *Keep Out!* extends not only to the general public and eagle-eyed UFO sleuths, but to the entire U.S. government as well. That's right: the aliens have complete control of the base, and anyone who dares to trespass upon their dark abode, from the president down, will receive nothing less than swift and fatal justice—and they may even become the victims of unspeakable genetic experimentation too.

At least, that is the incredible legend that has come to be believed by whole swathes of the UFO research community. But sorting fact from fiction in this infinitely weird and convoluted affair is no easy task.

The Facts

The saga of the Dulce base began in the late 1970s with a physicist named Paul Bennewitz, who, after digging into Air Force and National Security Agency (NSA) secret projects at Kirtland Air Force Base in New Mexico, came to believe that those projects were connected to the activities of sinister extraterrestrials and UFOs. It became all too easy for Bennewitz to focus his attention on such operations: Rather conveniently—much to the concern of the Air Force—his company, Thunder Scientific Labs, actually bordered on the perimeter of Kirtland itself.

It seems, however, that what Bennewitz had *really* tapped into was a wealth of classified projects connected to (a) NSA communications systems, (b) test flights, and maybe even crashes, of early prototype Stealth aircraft, and (c) Air Force technologies designed to secretly track the movements of spy satellites launched into Earth orbit by the former Soviet Union.

Unsurprisingly, the U.S. Intelligence community was far less worried by Bennewitz's UFO beliefs than it was concerned about his digging into their actual secret programs. There was a very real concern on the part of officialdom that in seeking to penetrate the covert operations of Kirtland in search of UFOs, Bennewitz would inadvertently reveal to the Russians information and technology that had to be kept hidden at all costs—even if those costs were destined to include Bennewitz's own sanity and health.

So, members of the Air Force broke into Bennewitz's home while he was out, and carefully read his computer files and research notes. They learned the essential parts of his theories: that aliens were mutilating cattle as part of some weird medical experiment; that aliens were abducting American citizens and implanting them with bizarre devices for purposes disturbingly unknown; that aliens were living deep underground in a secure fortress at Dulce; and that the entire human race was very soon going to be in deep and dire trouble as a direct result of the presence of an intergalactic threat. Then, the Air Force gave Bennewitz precisely what he was looking for: conjured-up confirmation that his theories were all terrifyingly true.

Bennewitz was duly bombarded with a mass of alien-themed disinformation, faked official documents, fictitious stories of cosmic horror, rumors of nightmarish underground facilities, and outright lies. This was, basically, a carefully planned ruse. Its goal was to swamp Bennewitz with so much bogus UFO data that it would steer him away from the conventional, classified military projects of a strictly non-UFO nature that he had uncovered at Kirtland Air Force Base. It worked. In fact, it all worked rather *too* well, and it led to the catastrophic mental, psychological, and physical disintegration of the physicist.

When Bennewitz received confirmation (albeit carefully controlled and utterly fabricated confirmation) that he had stumbled upon the horrible truth and that there really *was* an alien base deep below Dulce where imprisoned people were being experimented on in horrific fashion by cold-hearted aliens, he became increasingly disturbed, paranoid, and unstable. But he began looking *away* from Kirtland (the hub of the genuine military secrets that had to be kept secure, no matter what) and *towards* the vicinity of Dulce, where his actions, research, and theories could be carefully controlled and coldly manipulated by government agents.

Researcher Greg Bishop, who has studied the Bennewitz/Dulce controversy very deeply, has been careful to stress one particularly important factor on this matter: The Air Force's bone-chilling manipulation of Bennewitz doesn't necessarily rule out the possibility of a *real* underground installation existing somewhere in the region of Dulce. Instead, it means only that we should be extremely careful with the way we analyze and interpret the story and all its many attendant controversies. The tale of the underground base at Dulce is most certainly one that many within the UFO research community wish to hear—after all, it is filled with excitement, alien intrigue, and outrageous, possibly even manifestly illegal

UFO researcher Greg Bishop at the grave of
Dulce Base investigator Paul Bennewitz.

government shenanigans. But does that mean the entire
story of the underground alien installation at Dulce is
bogus? Were the stories of the base simply born out of
the fertile imaginations of government agents, as a means
to destabilize and frighten Paul Bennewitz to the point
where he gave up—or was forced to give up—his research
at Kirtland? Many actually believe not. One of the prime
reasons for that is simple: For decades, Dulce and its surrounding areas have been a hotbed of very strange activity.

On December 10, 1967, the Atomic Energy
Commission (AEC) detonated a 29-kiloton-yield nuclear
device 4,240 feet below ground level, in an attempt to
provoke the release and also production of natural gas.
Thus was born Gasbuggy, part of an overall project known
as Operation Plowshare, which, ostensibly, was designed

to explore the peaceful uses of atomic energy. Notably, the location of the Gasbuggy test—which covered an area of 640 acres—was New Mexico's Carson National Forest, which just happens to be situated only 12 miles from the town of Dulce.

For nine years, gas-production tests and project evaluation activities were conducted; the AEC finally decommissioned and closed the site in 1978. Equipment and structures utilized in the operation were then duly decontaminated, taken apart, and moved to the ultra-secret Department of Energy's (DoE) Nevada Test Site, which today is known as the Nevada National Security Site. Meanwhile, liquid-form, radioactive waste was dumped into the sizeable cavity that had been created by the nuclear blast, and test-wells were scrupulously sealed. Until 2002, diligent, periodic soil-sampling of the immediate area and its surroundings was undertaken by DoE personnel. And

Operation Plowshare: A program for the
peaceful use of atomic power.

the Environmental Protection Agency has, since 1972, annually monitored water supplies in the area, specifically to ensure there has been no local contamination—which, we are assured with confidence, there has not been.

Rather interestingly, strict laws exist in the vicinity of the Gasbuggy explosion, specifically warning against any and all extensive underground digging. In fact, a plaque at the site makes it very clear that there must be *no* sub-surface intrusion, whatsoever, within a radius of 600 feet from surface to ground zero to a vertical depth of between 1,500 and 4,500 feet without the specific per-mission of the U.S. government. Inevitably, and perhaps even understandably, this has led to suspicions that the *real* reason why the world of officialdom does not want people digging deep in and around the area is in case they stumble upon evidence of—or even entrance points to—the legendary underground alien base.

Cattle Mutilations

Underground detonations and alien base rumors aside, Dulce has also become notable for another rea-son—and it's one of a decidedly grisly nature. Between 1975 and 1978, the town of Dulce became a hotbed of reports of cattle mutilation, a gruesome activity that has plagued North America for more than four decades: An uninvited, unwelcome guest roams the countryside stealthily by night, performing terrible acts of mutilation on cattle. Organs, blood, and glands are removed in ways that suggest a superior technology is the culprit. In many instances of such mutilation, unidentified aerial lights are reported in the same locales, implying that the two occur-rences are somehow deeply interconnected.

Black, unmarked, military helicopters are also often seen in the vicinity of these mutilation incidents, and stories abound of witnesses being threatened into silence by dark, governmental forces. Who, or what, is responsible for these horrific acts of butchery is a topic that has provoked intense debate. Wild predators, devil-worshipping cults, UFOs, and covert biological-warfare operations undertaken by secret arms of the government have all been suggested as the guilty parties. The macabre mystery, meanwhile, continues to rage. And the mutilators silently continue without interruption.

For the men and women of the FBI assigned to deal with the cattle mutilations in and around Dulce in the 1970s, the first step was to review the files of Police Officer Gabe Valdez, of the nearby city of Española. Between August 1975 and the summer of 1978, almost 30 cases of cattle mutilation were recorded by Valdez in the Rio Arriba area, with many indicating that the attacks were the work of a well-equipped, highly advanced intelligence. One report, filed by Valdez in June 1976, stands out in particular. At 8 p.m. on June 13, Valdez was contacted by a rancher named Manuel Gomez and advised that Gomez had found a 3-year-old cow on his ranch that bore all the classic signs of mutilation. As Valdez listened carefully, Gomez stated that the cow's left ear, tongue, udder, and rectum had been removed with what appeared to be a sharp instrument. Yet there was absolutely no blood in the immediate vicinity of the cow, nor were any footprints in evidence. There were, however, marks of some sort...they were marks that gave every impression that some form of unknown aerial object had landed and carried out a grisly attack on the unfortunate animal.

At 5 a.m. on the following day, Valdez set off for the Gomez ranch, along with Paul Riley, of the New Mexico Cattle Sanitary Board. On arriving, Officer Valdez and Riley were confronted by a scene of complete carnage. The cow was just as Gomez had described, lying on its right side, vital body parts having been removed with the utmost precision. But that was not all. There were also strange landing marks. Valdez recorded the details in a two-page report written shortly afterward, now declassified by the FBI.

The document might have read like science fiction, but it was just about as far removed from fiction as you could imagine. Investigations at the site, led by Valdez, revealed that some form of aircraft had landed at least twice, in the process depositing three pod marks positioned in a triangular shape. Further, careful investigation at the scene demonstrated that the tripod markings had pursued the cow for approximately 600 feet. Other evidence showed that grass around the areas on which the tripods had landed was inexplicably and significantly scorched. Also, a yellow-colored, oily substance was located in two places under the small tripod patterns. On this latter point, Valdez wrote in his report that the substance was dispatched to a forensic lab of the New Mexico State Police. The outcome? The staff was unable to offer any meaningful explanation regarding the nature of the substance.

Three days later, Valdez contacted Dr. Howard Burgess, a retired scientist from Sandia Laboratories, and asked him to conduct a radiation test at the scene. The results were astounding. All around the tripod marks and in the immediate tracks, the radiation count was twice that of normal. Valdez came up with an intriguing hypothesis for this revelation: It was his opinion that someone was deliberately leaving the radiation traces as part of a concerted effort to confuse and hinder those working to resolve the cattle mutilation controversy.

Valdez discovered something else too. In the days between his first visit to the Gomez ranch and his second visit with Dr. Howard Burgess, the mysterious aerial object had returned. This led to a distressing discovery: "There was also evidence that the tripod marks had returned and removed the left ear. Tripod marks were found over Mr. Gomez's tire tracks of his original visit. The left ear was intact when Mr. Gomez first found the cow. The cow had a 3-month-old calf which has not been located since the incident. This appears strange since a small calf normally stays around the mother even though the cow is dead."[1]

Valdez noted in his report that this incident was typical of those he had investigated throughout the course of a 16-month period. Perhaps most pertinent, Valdez had been able to determine that in at least one case, the animal in question was found to have a high dose of a particular tranquilizing agent in its bloodstream. There was also major concern on the part of Valdez that government-associated laboratories were not reporting complete findings on the controversy. For that reason, Valdez ensured that samples from the slain cattle were later submitted to private chemists for separate, independent analysis. Valdez was fully aware of the theories that all of the mutilations were the work of either satanic cults or natural predators, but he dismissed them: "Both [theories] have been ruled out due to expertise and preciseness and the cost involved to conduct such a sophisticated and secretive operation.

It should also be noted that during the spring of 1974 when a tremendous amount of cattle were lost due to heavy snowfalls, the carcasses had been eaten by predators. These carcasses did not resemble the carcasses of the mutilated cows."[2]

Another FBI document from May 1978, the content of which is also based upon the investigations of Valdez, refers to a second incident when abnormal radiation traces were found: "It is believed that this type of radiation is not harmful to humans, although approximately seven people who visited the mutilation site complained of nausea and headaches. However, this writer has had no such symptoms after checking approximately 11 mutilations in the past four months. Identical mutilations have been taking place all over the Southwest. It is strange that no eyewitnesses have come forward or that no accidents [have] occurred. One has to admit that whoever is responsible for the mutilations is very well organized, with boundless financing and secrecy."[3]

Strange landing-marks, elevated radiation readings, and tranquilizing drugs...upon what had Officer Valdez stumbled? Was this a highly secret government-sponsored or military-controlled operation, perhaps centered on germ-warfare testing, or maybe something even more bizarre? FBI documentation generated as a direct result of Valdez's police reports suggests that the Bureau took very seriously the evidence and official testimony that the officer had collected: "Officer Valdez stated that Colorado probably has the most mutilations occurring within their State and that over the past four years approximately 30 have occurred in New Mexico. He stated that of these 30, 15 have occurred on Indian Reservations but he did know that many mutilations have gone unreported which have occurred on the Indian reservations because the Indians, particularly in the Pueblos, are extremely superstitious and will not even allow officers in to investigate in some instances. Officer Valdez stated since the outset of these mutilations there have been an estimated 8,000 animals mutilated which would place the loss at approximately $1,000,000."[4]

Armed with a $50,000 grant, a three-person team led by Director Kenneth M. Rommel, Jr., who had served with the FBI for 28 years, began investigations. To the surprise of no one who viewed the study as little more than a whitewash, Rommel found very little out of the ordinary. In fact, he found *absolutely nothing* out of the ordinary. By the summer of 1980, he had prepared a final, extensive, bound report entitled "Operation Animal Mutilation," copies of which were circulated throughout the FBI. The final entry in the FBI's cattle-mutilation file sums up Rommel's conclusions: "A perusal of this report reflects it adds nothing new with regard to potential investigation by the Albuquerque FBI of alleged mutilations on Indian lands in New Mexico."[5] The door on the cattle-mutilations of Dulce was quietly and decisively closed. So we are told, anyway.

Were the cattle killings really due to the regular predations of normal wild predators? Were they the work of military personnel engaged in strange biological warfare experimentation? Or might they have been caused by malevolent aliens, covertly surfacing after sunset from their cavernous underground abode at nearby Dulce, and engaging in a liberal amount of nightmarish genetic experimentation? Was it only a coincidence that, with its Gasbuggy program, the Department of Energy just happened to have been blasting deep underground in the 1960s, in the very same area where it was said the extraterrestrials were hiding out in the 1970s? Was the purpose behind Gasbuggy actually wholly different from what we have been told? Incredibly, might it really have been a Top Secret attempt by an utterly panicked U.S. government to destroy the underground alien base with a powerful nuclear device, before the intruders from the stars became unstoppable in their apocalyptic agenda?

○

It is precisely these questions that, more than 30 years after Paul Bennewitz began focusing his attentions on Dulce, have kept alive the controversy surrounding the alleged alien installation beneath the little New Mexican town. The controversy shows no signs of stopping either. In fact, the stories concerning Dulce's underground nightmare have become progressively more and more extreme and outlandish as the years have advanced. Since the mid-1980s—by which time the government's black-hearted actions had reduced Paul Bennewitz to a shell of his former self—a wealth of outrageous stories have surfaced suggesting that the true nature of the underground alien base at Dulce is far more horrific than had previously been suggested or even imagined.

Nightmare Hall

An author going by the pseudonym of "Branton" wrote of a shadowy individual named Thomas Castello, who claimed to have had access to the Dulce base and to inside information on diabolical medical experiments undertaken by the aliens on both human and animal captives. Branton's source said that deep inside what was allegedly known as Nightmare Hall, supposedly just one part of a vast, multi-leveled facility under Archuleta Peak: "Experiments [are] done on fish, seals, birds and mice that are vastly altered from their original forms. There are multi-armed and multi-legged humans and several cages of bat-like creatures up to seven feet tall.... I frequently encountered humans in cages, usually dazed or drugged, but sometimes they cried for help."[6]

Wild and controversial stuff, to be sure; however, the data came from an author using an alias, who in turn secured it from a source that has been unable to offer definitive proof of his testimony, which effectively renders the tale useless in terms of offering us hard evidence in support of the theory that the Dulce base really exists.

Alien Occupation

As the 1980s progressed and ultimately became the 1990s, the stories mutated even more. Suggestions that diminutive aliens with large bald heads and black eyes—the so-called "Grays" of UFO lore and popular culture—in the company of vicious, bipedal, reptilian entities, were entirely running the base with a lethal, iron-grip, took hold within the UFO research arena. As did widely circulated tales to the effect that, in 1979, a veritable infantry of highly trained U.S. military personnel stormed the base, in an effort to try to wipe out the alien hordes once and for all. The story goes that the operation was a catastrophic failure, and what was left of the Delta Force–style team made a hasty retreat after suffering defeat, countless casualties, and a large number of fatalities.

Since then, rumors persist that the government has been reluctantly forced to keep a considerable distance, all the while quietly trying to figure out a permanent way to rid the Earth of the alien threat, and destroy its cavernous home far beneath New Mexico.

To what extent any of these admittedly outrageous claims and tales have a basis in fact is anybody's guess. They may merely be the latest in a series of lies and half-truths spread by the Intelligence community, in a fashion similar to the way Paul Bennewitz was psychologically pummeled in the late 1970s. Whatever the case, the Dulce specter still continues to loom in the 21st century almost as large as Archuleta Mesa itself.

On March 29, 2009, the first Underground Base Conference was held in the area, and it attracted a packed audience, all eager to hear the full scoop on what was really going on deep beneath them. Then, in January 2010, a researcher named Anthony Sanchez spoke with a retired U.S. Air Force operative who confirmed the reality of the Dulce facility. But that was not all: Sanchez's source advised him that rather than there being just one secret base, there were actually *three* underground facilities in the area: one, as has long been rumored, below Archuleta Mesa, which is said to be code-named TA-D1; a second, two-story complex, dubbed TA-D2, built close to the Colorado state line; and a third base, TA-D3, located in the Leandro Canyon, which, interestingly enough, is very close to the Project Gasbuggy test site of 1967. Sanchez was advised that "T.A." is an abbreviation for "Technical Area."

Notably, Sanchez's (unsurprisingly) unnamed colonel asserted that no one named Thomas Castello had ever been employed in connection with the Dulce facilities, and that the stories of malevolent, reptilian aliens prowling around the depths of New Mexico were utterly bogus. Interestingly, however, the colonel *did* confirm the reality of the disastrous 1979 altercation between elements of the U.S. military and what he vaguely described as certain other inhabitants of the Dulce base.

Essentially, that is where matters stand to this day. Although many within the UFO research community scoff at what sounds like the script for some mega-scale movie, the story refuses to roll over and die. What is really going on beneath Dulce, New Mexico?

Remote Viewing

The town of Dulce may not be alone when it comes to the controversy of secret alien bases in the United States. The details are unfortunately scant, but a somewhat similar story—also from the 1970s—came from the late Pat Price, who, before his untimely and sudden death in 1974, was one of the U.S. government's most successful psychic spies. In the early 1970s, elements of the Intelligence community, including the CIA, U.S. Army Intelligence, and the Defense Intelligence Agency, explored such controversial areas as extrasensory perception (ESP) and psychic phenomena, with a specific view to determining if such mental powers could be utilized as a means to spy on the former Soviet Union. The results were decidedly mixed, but Price proved to be a highly successful remote-viewer, as such spies became known.

One of the more unsettling things that Price reportedly uncovered, via psychic means, was the existence of a huge alien base hidden deep inside Alaska's Mount Hayes, the highest mountain in the eastern Alaskan Range. According to Price's findings, the aliens were very human-looking, aside from exhibiting certain differences in their heart, lungs, blood, and eyes. More disturbing, the E.T.s were said to be using advanced psychic powers to control certain elements of the populace—for purposes unknown, but suspected of being manifestly sinister in nature and intent. This surely begs an important question: How many *more* secret, Dulce-like alien bases might there be across our world, carefully hidden from prying human eyes, and possibly even inaccessible to worried governments, utterly powerless to stop a spreading, extraterrestrial infestation?

C - 9

A
LAND
DOWN
UNDER

UNLIKE THE UNITED STATES, RUSSIA, AND China, Australia is, for a country with a land mass of nearly three million square miles, remarkably and refreshingly free of government-designated no-fly zones. With one exception. No, it's not the airspace above the nation's capital, Canberra. Nor, as you might expect, is it the skies directly over the residence of the current Australian Prime Minister, Julia Gillard. Rather, the flight-free area in question protects the staff and work of a highly classified installation previously called the Joint Defense Space Research Facility, now officially titled the Joint Defense Facility Pine Gap. To most Aussies, however, it's referred to simply as Pine Gap.

Situated in central Australia, about 11 miles from the town of Alice Springs, Pine Gap is an area dominated by dry, arid grassland, with temperatures that, in the summer, regularly reach nearly 100 degrees Fahrenheit. It is described in careful terms by the Australian government as a satellite-tracking station—which it is, but it's also far, far more than that. It's a place that would likely have given George Orwell nightmares. That's right: Feeds from spy cameras in overseas nations and around their own country end up in the heart of Pine Gap—secret surveillance of worldwide targets as well as elements of the Australian populace deemed to be targets of interest, which in today's world may include genuine homegrown terrorists, but can also involve everyday citizens grousing about the ever-increasing number of state-of-the-art surveillance cameras popping up across the nation's cities.

The origins of the facility can be traced back to 1966, the year in which the governments of Australia and the United States of America secretly signed what has become known as the Pine Gap Treaty. In simple terms, it allowed for the establishment, on Australian soil, of a highly classified eavesdropping facility that, for the most part, would be manned by personnel from the U.S. NSA and CIA. And that is precisely what happened: At the dawn of the 1970s, hundreds of Americans employed in the secret worlds of intelligence-gathering and espionage made their quiet way to Australia, to a brand-new facility equipped with the latest state-of-the-art surveillance equipment and technologies.

Today, vast radomes—protective enclosures for radar antennae—dominate the base, giving it an otherworldly appearance. Its number of employees is now rumored to

Huge radomes, similar to the type that
exist at Pine Gap, Australia.

be close to a thousand. Top Secret operations involving
spy satellites, telephone and Internet surveillance, and sophisticated, clandestine means of eavesdropping at both a
foreign and a domestic level are the norm. In a somewhat
surreal situation, given that the base is on Australian soil,
all Australian employees of Pine Gap are legally unable to
access one part of the installation known as the National
Cryptographic Room, which falls under U.S. jurisdiction. And, by the same token, U.S. personnel are denied
access to the Australian Cryptographic Room. Both are
said to secretly spy on each others' rooms, however.

Much of the work undertaken at Pine Gap is undeniably done in the legitimate name of national security,
and focuses upon such areas as terror threats, determining if foreign nations are abiding by arms-control trea-
ties, and intelligence-gathering. But, as the Age of Terror
progresses, concerns are rising that a significant portion
of the work at Pine Gap is now based around watching
Australia's own law-abiding citizens, rather than just

those overseas individuals and groups who might wish
to do the nation and its people harm. For example, in
2010, a Pine Gap whistleblower revealed that the base
was involved in the secret monitoring of telephone and
e-mail activities of Australian citizens attached to animal-
rights movements, the Global Warming community, and
the 9/11 Truth Movement. Not surprisingly, issues like
this have led more than a few people to make their outrage known. One of the most notable aspects of the complaints about the work undertaken at Pine Gap is that
they do not come from overseas nations, angered that
their actions are being monitored to an intensive degree,
but from the Australian people themselves, who have
proven to be highly proactive when it comes to the issue
of highlighting, and demonstrating against, what may
very well be going on behind the heavily guarded doors
of the secret base.

When Pine Gap celebrated its 20th anniversary in
1986, there was no party, no birthday cake, and no candles.
Instead, Pine Gap personnel were faced with the sight of
more than 300 women demonstrating outside the base,
before they stormed the facility (and were quickly arrested
in the process). Anxious to play down the affair, authorities quickly and quietly dropped all charges. It was much
the same in 2002, when no less than 500 people loudly
protested on the perimeter of the installation about Pine
Gap's escalating involvement in the War on Terror, and
the extent to which Australia was getting dragged into
the controversial hostilities seemingly erupting all across
the Middle East. For the most part, the demonstrators
made their point and went on their collective way. As the
hostilities in Iraq and Afghanistan continued to grow,
however, strong-arm tactics began to surface.

The one case that, more than any other, thrust the work of Pine Gap into the public domain had its origins in December 2005, when four members—Adele Goldie, Jim Dowling, Donna Mulhearn, and Bryan Law—of a group called Christians Against all Terrorism found their way into the base. In what was certainly a unique scenario, the four had publicly announced, *in advance*, that it was their intention to enter the base and inspect the extent to which staff at Pine Gap were assisting in the enabling and targeting of missiles engaged in the bombing of Iraq and Afghanistan. Unsurprisingly, all four were arrested before they had a chance to take a breath. This time, however, there was no attempt to release the protestors and sweep the events under a thick carpet of diplomacy. This time, the Australian government meant business.

Asserting his position of authority, Attorney General Philip Ruddock quickly invoked a seldom-used law to prosecute all four: the Defense (Special Undertaking) Act of 1952. If convicted of violating the law, the four faced serving 14 years in jail—seven for trespass and a further seven for taking unauthorized photographs of the installation. And you thought security at Area 51 was tough. Potentially even more serious, however: the 1952 act also provided the government with nearly unlimited powers to take action in events relevant to the purposes of the defense of the Commonwealth. In other words, provided it successfully argued that its actions were in the name of the defense of the nation, the Australian government could pretty much do whatever it wanted to do.

The legal counsel for the four came up with an argument that many saw as quite logical when the case finally went to trial in 2007. The Defense (Special Undertaking)

Act specifically—as its name implies—covers issues of a *defensive* nature; the argument put forth by the four's defense was that the actions at Pine Gap were perceived by the members of Christians Against all Terrorism as not being defensive. Instead, the argument went, Pine Gap was involved in *offensive* acts—namely, offering intelligence data that assisted in the military attacks on overseas nations such as Iraq and Afghanistan.

Justice Sally Thomas, however, was having none of it. Had she accepted the argument, it would have set a very dangerous precedent from the government's perspective: Much of Pine Gap's work is focused on spying on foreign nations, and it could be argued in future cases that, by definition, spying on the enemy overseas is not, technically speaking, defensive. Therefore, invoking the 1952 legislation would not just be pointless, it would be illegal too. Even though the government knew full well that the defense's argument was not exactly an invalid one, the case was not thrown out of court. In fact, Goldie, Dowling, Mulhearn and Law and were successfully prosecuted to the full extent to which officialdom was conceivably able.

Although the prosecution team strived for—and the government secretly yearned for—the four to serve prison time, it was not to be. Collectively, they received fines totaling only $3,500—which they flatly refused to pay. An utterly exasperated Australian government pushed to overturn the verdict and punishment and put all four behind bars at the earliest opportunity—like *right now*. Well, that didn't work either. What *did* happen was that the legal team for Goldie, Dowling, Mulhearn and Law quickly launched an appeal, and, remarkably, got the entire conviction quashed and nullified, as a result of concerns relative to the perceived unconstitutional way in which the act of 1952 had been introduced, interpreted, and used against the four. While the foursome celebrated their freedom, the government quietly seethed. The secret work of Pine Gap continued on behind closed doors.

UFOS

Pine Gap has been linked to matters of a much stranger nature than covert intelligence-gathering, however: More than a few UFO reports have surfaced from this area. Since the early to mid-1970s, eyewitnesses have described seeing strange balls of bright light hovering over the base; gleaming, saucer-shaped aircraft have been seen soaring across the surrounding land; and, according to an Australian university professor named J.D. Frodsham, on one particular night in 1989, a hunting party in the area secretly watched as a set of camouflaged doors opened in the grounds of Pine Gap, out of which surfaced a metallic-looking, circular-shaped vehicle that rose vertically and then sped away into the night sky.

Combined with the fact that Pine Gap was previously known as the Joint Defense Space Research Facility, incredible stories such as these have inevitably given rise to the notion that a secret alien base—perhaps not unlike that which is allegedly buried below the town of Dulce, New Mexico—exists underneath Pine Gap. Although, given the current status of the highly advanced technology employed at Pine Gap, one might conclude that the UFOs are, in reality, classified vehicles of a very terrestrial nature: Perhaps they may actually be surveillance craft not unlike the remotely piloted vehicles (RPVs) or unmanned aerial vehicles (UAVs) now being flown in the skies of the Middle East. If so, as seems to be the case at Area 51, Pine Gap personnel might prefer and even encourage people to believe such vehicles have alien origins. Either way, from the depths of the Nevada desert to the Australian interior, it seems, secret bases and UFOs, whatever their point of origin, go hand-in-glove.

CREATURES
OF
THE
CAVES

c - 10

OF THE MANY MULTIFACETED THEORIES THAT have been advanced to try and explain what lies at the heart of the UFO puzzle, one of the most controversial suggests that, rather than representing intruders from far-away star systems, the assumed aliens are really the last vestiges of a very ancient—but very terrestrial—race of advanced entities that originated right here on Earth. They have either chosen or have been forced to live outside of human society, within huge, cavernous underworlds far beneath the surface of our planet.

As this theory goes, our presumed aliens are intimately related to Homo sapiens at a genetic level, to the extent that their close physical similarities allow them to stealthily move among us—with the aid of a few carefully prepared props to obscure their real appearances, such as wrap-around shades, wigs, pulled-down hats, upturned collars, and makeup. Our leaders are said to secretly know all about these ancient people. They know these curious entities are the original masters of the world that we have claimed as our own, which we are increasingly infesting, plundering, and ravaging. And officialdom is also keenly aware that nothing can be done to prevent these beings from meddling in and carefully manipulating our lives to suit their own potentially sinister purposes and agendas.

Such a scenario is without doubt an ominous one. Imagine this: You're walking home late one night. The air is eerily still and the moon is full. As you approach your front door you feel a distinct chill, and you see a curious little fellow eyeing you carefully from across the street. Stranger still, via the light coming from a nearby streetlamp, you can see he's wearing an old-fashioned fedora hat and a long black coat. And he looks deathly pale too. Menacingly zombie-like, even. Maybe he's not, as your mind had quickly assumed, just some weirdo out for a late-night stroll, or even, worse still a deranged mugger. Perhaps he's actually one of a veritable army of underworld intruders that have wormed their secret way into our cities, weaving plans under cover of darkness and shadow for the day when they reclaim the world that was once all theirs. Is such a scenario just too crazy for words? You'd better hope it is, or one day we could all be in deep, dire trouble.

The deep caverns of our world are said to be populated by strange, unearthly creatures (such as this model monster).

close encounters

Before we get to the matter of what our leaders may know about this hidden society and its secret underground abode, it's first necessary to note that encounters with unusual entities from the world below us are surprisingly common. One of the most macabre accounts that falls into this particular category occurred in 1942 at a reportedly haunted mine in Arizona. Paranormal investigator Brad Steiger says of this tale, "According to local legends, the mine had been abandoned when the miners [ran] into some sort of cave. From that moment on, ill fortune plagued those miners. Portions of the tunnel caved in, crushing several miners. A couple of the investors in the mine died as a result of strange accidents, and a number of the miners simply disappeared without a trace."[1]

The idea of a haunted mine might very well keep superstitious miners at bay, but for two teenage boys who had heard the legends of the mine, the lure of adventure in that underground maze of tunnels was too appealing. So it was that in the summer of 1942 the intrepid lads elected to seek out the inner depths of the deep, dark mine for themselves. It was an action that proved costly, as Brad Steiger notes: "[They] passed the deserted buildings of the mining camp and climbed over a large pile of debris located at one side of the mine entrance. It was there, standing as if on guard at the mine opening, that the boys saw the grotesque monster. About four and a half feet tall, but very thick in bulk, the being let out an unearthly scream and started around the edge of the mine toward the boys."[2]

Both fled in absolute terror. Curiously, years later one of the boys (by then an adult) stated that after fleeing the mine, he hid out in a local movie theater, only to be horrified by dark and menacing figures that were walking up and down the dimly lit aisle, seemingly searching for him. But that was not all: On retiring to his bed that night, the boy felt certain that he caught a glimpse of a hideous dark form squatting on a high limb of a tree near his home, staring intently in his direction. Was the presence of the ominous entity a warning, perhaps, to the boy to keep away from the old mine and its underground secrets? We may never know.

The Shaver Mystery

As the 1940s progressed, so did the astounding tales. Or, more to the point, so did the "amazing stories." Ray

Palmer, the editor of the legendary *Amazing Stories* magazine from 1938 to 1949, had a hell of a hard time as a kid. At the age of 7, he was involved in a violent collision with a truck that shattered his spine, which significantly stunted his growth and provoked endless health issues throughout his life. None of us, unless we have personally undergone such a traumatic event, can begin to imagine how we might react to such a situation in our formative years. Maybe we would do precisely what the young Palmer did: He became somewhat reclusive as a result of cruel taunts from local kids and ignorant adults. From the solitude of his bedroom, Palmer buried his head deeply within the pages of the science-fiction magazines of the 1920s and 30s. If the real world was just too much for the damaged Palmer to deal with, then the realm of futuristic fantasy would have to take its place. In the final year of his teens Palmer started co-editing his very own fanzine, titled the *Comet*, which was enthusiastically welcomed by the burgeoning science-fiction community of the day. But the biggest event in Palmer's life came in 1938. It was a veritable dream come true.

Ziff-Davis, the publisher of *Amazing Stories* magazine, had just moved its base of operations from the Big Apple to the Windy City, and, in the process, dumped its editor, T. O'Connor-Sloane. As Palmer didn't live too far away—in the heart of Milwaukee—and Ziff-Davis knew of his *Comet* publication, an offer was made to Palmer that he could not refuse: a full-time gig as the editor of *Amazing Stories*.

Today, Palmer's position as head honcho of *Amazing Stories* is remembered, chiefly, for two specific reasons:

1. He bought and published Isaac Asimov's very first professional science-fiction story, titled "Marooned off Vesta."

2. He became the leading light in a decidedly odd affair that became known as the Shaver Mystery.

Whether the Shaver saga was science fiction or science fact is a matter that still has people guessing.

The Shaver Mystery had its origins at the height of the Second World War. It was a relatively normal day in 1943 when Palmer was opening the daily delivery of mail that regularly poured into the offices of *Amazing Stories*, and came across one particular missive penned by a certain Richard Shaver. "Weird" barely begins to describe it. Shaver wrote that he personally had uncovered a sensational and terrifying secret: In our distant past a race of ancient, highly evolved entities lived right under our very feet. Massive caverns, huge caves, and endless tunnels were the dark, damp places they called home.

At least, that is, before they decided to exit the Earth and head away to a new world on the other side of the galaxy. When these particular entities said their final goodbyes to our planet, they left behind them something truly sinister and abominable: their diseased, mentally deranged offspring, which were said to be called the Deros. Taunting the human race, finding more and more ways to screw up our lives and plague our minds, and, even worse, using us as food, were just some of their bad habits. Yes, according to Shaver, human beings were being systematically kidnapped and devoured by cave-dwelling grotesqueries.

For Palmer, this nightmare scenario looked like fun; as the astute editor of *Amazing Stories*, he quickly grasped the significance and potential enormity of the story that had fallen into his lap. He knew the story would highly entertain his readers, and probably wouldn't hurt sales figures either. History has proven Palmer correct on those counts.

But before he could proceed any further, Palmer realized that he needed much more from Shaver. Important questions needing answering: had Shaver been to this terrifying underworld? Might he even have personally encountered the deadly, psychotic Deros? If not, then from where was Shaver getting his information? This is where things got even more warped. Shaver eagerly wrote back to Palmer with the answers to his questions, and I suspect they were not the ones he was expecting.

Shaver wrote that, in 1932, he was employed as a welder in a car factory, where most days were routine. But one day most certainly was not: On the occasion in question, wrote Shaver, his welding gun began talking to him. It did so, said Shaver, "by some freak of its coil's field attunements."[3] Then, telepathically delivered tales of a horrific nature were beamed into what amounted to Shaver's mind, all relative to the Deros, their penchant for human meat, and their underground cities. Shaver was so pleased by Palmer's quick reply to his original missive that he penned a 10,000-word story that detailed the salient points of the affair, including the outrageous claim that he, Shaver, had been the captive of the Deros for a number of years prior to making good his escape.

This was absolutely great for Palmer, who duly burned the midnight oil, tidying up and editing Shaver's story, which finally appeared in *Amazing Stories* in March 1945, in a feature titled "I Remember Lemuria." Sales of that particular issue bypassed the roof and went through the stratosphere, and both Palmer and the publisher were delighted. Neither, however, was quite prepared for the thousands of letters that poured into the offices of *Amazing Stories* from a multitude of readers who had become fascinated by the tales of Richard Shaver. *We want more*—those were the words coming from the huge readership, and Palmer did not disappoint. The Shaver controversy continued for decades, constantly being added to by other characters who claimed knowledge of the Deros and their evil underworld. Today, the entire issue is viewed by the majority of UFO researchers as nothing more than a practical joke initiated by Shaver and then expanded upon by Palmer, ever ready to increase the audience of his cherished magazine, no matter how tall the tale was.

However, others have told similar, more credible stories of these underground creatures.

Mac Tonnies

Author Mac Tonnies, right up until the point of his tragic passing in October 2009 at the age of 34, was hot on the trail of these ancient, underground humanoids, which he chose to call the Cryptoterrestrials. Tonnies told me, only a couple of months before his death, "After devouring countless books on the UFO controversy and the paranormal, I began to acknowledge that the extraterrestrial hypothesis suffered [from] some tantalizing flaws. In short, the 'aliens' seemed more like surreal caricatures of ourselves than beings possessing the god-like technology one might plausibly expect from interstellar visitors.

I came to the realization that the extraterrestrial hypothesis isn't strange enough to encompass the entirety of occupant cases."[4]

So, if E.T. wasn't weird enough for Tonnies, then what was? The under-dwellers, that's what. "If we're dealing with humanoid beings that evolved here on Earth," Tonnies said, "some of the problems vanish. I envision the Cryptoterrestrials engaged in a process of subterfuge, bending our belief systems to their own ends. And I suggest that this has been occurring, in one form or another, for an extraordinarily long time. I think there's a good deal of folkloric and mythological evidence pointing in this direction, and I find it most interesting that so many descriptions of ostensible 'aliens' seem to reflect staged events designed to misdirect witnesses and muddle their perceptions."[5]

official knowledge

We've now heard many civilian accounts, but what is known at an official level about these alleged ancient beings and their subterranean domains? The previously mentioned former U.S. Air Force Intelligence operative, Walter Bosley, made a highly valuable contribution toward answering this question. Bosley's father served in the U.S. Air Force in the late 1950s, and worked on matters relative to the U.S. space program. Significantly, during the period of his employment with the military, Bosley Sr. received at Wright-Patterson Air Force Base in Ohio—perhaps within the confines of the legendary Hangar 18—a classified briefing relative to the reported UFO crash at Roswell, New Mexico, in the summer of 1947.

Bosley said that by the time of his father's briefing, the Air Force had come to a startling conclusion: Neither the strange aerial device nor the bodies found in the desert outside of Roswell at the time in question had alien origins. His father told him the entities and their craft come from *inside* our planet. Their civilization supposedly resides within a huge underground system of caverns and tunnels beneath the southwest portion of the United States. Bosley was additionally told by his father that "They are human in appearance; so much so that they can move among us with ease with just a little effort. If you get a close look, you'd notice something odd, but not if the person just passed you on the street."[6]

Caves of conspiracy and nightmare.

We also have the illuminating tale of Nick Pope, who, for three years—from 1991 to 1994—officially investigated UFO encounters for the British Ministry of Defense (MoD). In 1999, Pope wrote a science-fiction novel titled *Operation Thunder Child*, which told of an alien invasion of the Earth from the perspective of the MoD and the British government. Notably, in Pope's novel, the U.S. government tells British officials that the aliens are nothing less than an offshoot of Neanderthal Man that, quite literally, went underground millennia ago, "developing their own complex social structures and technologies."[7]

At one point in Pope's book, the U.S. president confides in the British prime minister that these ancient humans "have been keeping a careful watch on our development, especially since the Industrial Revolution. But it's our progress in the last hundred years that has most frightened them."[8] As Pope's novel progresses, however, we learn that the truth is somewhat different: The ancient human angle, as presented to British officials, is really a U.S.-created ruse to mask a genuine extraterrestrial presence on our world.

This leaves us with a couple of thought-provoking questions: did Nick Pope, as a former UFO investigator for the Ministry of Defense, hear whispers and rumors from American friends and colleagues in the world of officialdom of the theory that our alien visitors may not be from faraway star systems, after all? If so, did he then choose to weave certain aspects of this scenario into his 1999 novel? The story of the alleged underworld inhabitants of our planet, it seems, is as winding and as shadowy as the tunnels and caves in which they are reputed to secretly dwell.

C-11

CITIES ON THE MOON

THUS FAR, ALL OF THE TOP SECRET locations discussed within the pages of this book can be found right here on Earth—as you would expect! But what about the *very* controversial issue of super-classified, off-planet facilities? Is it really feasible that our very own Moon, for example, is a secret haven for one or more highly advanced fortified bases of the U.S. government and/or military? Or, incredibly, might it be home to alien installations, the existence of which the official world is determined to keep buried at all costs, for fear of public panic and hysteria? Presently available data and testimony suggests the astonishing answer may very well be the affirmative—to both scenarios.

Hidden Moon Bases

In 1965, Karl Wolfe, an employee of the U.S. Air Force, was assigned to a project at Virginia's Langley Air Force Base that was linked to NASA's lunar-orbiter project. On one particularly memorable occasion, while speaking with a fellow airman, Wolfe was told that NASA had discovered something truly astounding while studying photographs of the Moon: a huge installation of unknown origins on the surface of the far side of the Moon. The photographs, Wolfe was informed, displayed clearly delineated buildings and structures that, collectively, were suggestive of a gigantic facility built by forces disturbingly unknown.

Wolfe, quickly realizing he had just been given details of a matter that certainly had major implications for national security, rapidly brought the conversation to a

Top Secret bases on the far side of the Moon? Many say: Yes!

close, even though, by his own admission, it amazed and fascinated him. Many people have concluded that Karl Wolfe's revelations are a very strong indication that aliens have secretly claimed our Moon as their own, and have begun the first, covert steps toward the colonization of our nearest heavenly neighbor via the construction of a secret base. Outrageous? Certainly! Impossible? Perhaps not. There is, however, a far more down-to-earth explanation for the existence of the strange space-city about which Karl Wolfe was informed.

It so transpires that as far back as the late 1950s the U.S. Army had a secret plan to build an outpost on the Moon: an impressively sized, permanently manned base that would demonstrate decisive military superiority over the former Soviet Union. And guess what: the Army's goal was to have the initial stages of the program in place by 1965—the very same year that Karl Wolfe was told that NASA had uncovered evidence of some form of intelligently designed installation on the far side of the Moon.

Even though the Army's operation—code-named *Project Horizon*—was reportedly canceled due to a lack of (a) adequate technology and (b) sufficient funding to achieve such a task nearly half a century ago, there are those who believe the project may not have been aborted at all, but secretly continued in stealth. In that case, the military may have a super-secret space program about which NASA knows very little, or possibly even nothing at all. Is such a scenario just too incredible to be true? Maybe it isn't.

On March 20, 1959, Lieutenant General Arthur G. Trudeau, Chief of Research and Development with the

U.S. Army, signed off on an extensive document that proposed the establishment (at a cost of approximately $6 billion) of an outpost on the Moon, constructed and controlled by the Army. Thus was born Project Horizon. In the opening pages of the several-hundred-page report, titled "Project Horizon: A U.S. Army Study for the Establishment of a Lunar Military Outpost," Trudeau wrote, "There is a requirement for a manned military outpost on the Moon. The lunar outpost is required to develop and protect potential United States interests on the Moon; to develop techniques in Moon-based surveillance of the earth and space, in communications relay, and in operations on the surface of the Moon; to serve as a base for exploration of the Moon, for further exploration into space and for military operations on the Moon if required; and to support scientific investigations on the Moon."[1]

The plan was manifestly ambitious, and it soon became even more so: Wernher von Braun—at the time, the head of the Army Ballistic Missile Agency—appointed Heinz-Hermann Koelle, a brilliant aeronautical engineer, to oversee the project. It was then that plans began in earnest. The Project Horizon documentation notes that, initially at least, any such installation would have to be relatively small, housing 10 to 20 people at any given time. Nevertheless, the authors of the report stressed the importance of constructing the base in a fashion that would allow for it to be constantly expanded upon in size and scope, and eventually even allowing for a considerable presence to eventually be maintained on a permanent basis. It was clearly recognized that such a base would have allowed the United States to massively increase its scientific knowledge of the Moon and the new and expanding domain of space, but it was without doubt the military potential of the Moon that was deemed so important to America's long-term goals.

Clearly realizing it was practically inevitable that space would one day become militarized, the Project Horizon team speculated that the Army's emergency communications systems would greatly benefit from having a relay station on the Moon, in the event of some form of national emergency—such as an atomic attack by the Soviet Union—that might take out ground communication systems on Earth. As a result, plans were formulated—in a worst-case scenario—to vigorously defend the base with nuclear weapons against Communist attack.

Staff even anticipated the startling scenario of Russian soldiers—in full cosmonaut gear—reaching the secret Moon base and doing battle with U.S. Army personnel, as part of a concerted effort to either destroy the facility or capture it and place it under Soviet control. In a section of the report titled "Degree of Urgency," it was made abundantly clear that one of the main aims of Project Horizon was to reach the Moon and establish an outpost before the Soviets did.

Army personnel outlined the extensive and rigorous training procedures that Army astronauts would need to follow when faced with living on the Moon for weeks or even months at any given time, as well as the means by which oxygen and water could be extracted from the Moon's natural environment, to ensure the base could be maintained and inhabited at all times. Demonstrating the amount of thought the Project Horizon team had given to this aspect of the ground-breaking venture, reference was made to the possibility that the Moon might very well be rich in minerals and other materials that could successfully be mined and made commercially available.

Any such fantastic, clandestine operation would require a massive amount of planning, forward-thinking, and dedication to the task at hand. The program's staff envisaged that the materials required in the construction of the lunar colony could be shuttled, piece by piece, to the Moon via huge, multi-stage rockets (and possibly even in conjunction with the use of huge orbiting space stations).

As for the base itself, it might very well have been advantageous, the report reveals, to carefully remodel a natural cavern on the Moon and into an environment suitable for the sustainment of the initial team. Such a program of construction, it was estimated, could begin by 1965 and would likely involve a two-person team flying to a specific location on the Moon where materials would have already been deposited via previously dispatched cargo craft. Chiefly, the facility would be constructed out of interlocking metal tanks, 20 feet in length and 10 feet in diameter, the first of which constituting the living quarters of the initial construction team. Astonishingly, those working on Project Horizon estimated that the base—albeit in small, rudimentary form—could be up and running within as little as two weeks after the arrival of the cargo and the crews.

It might be useful, opined those who prepared the Project Horizon documentation, to have the interconnecting cylinders buried underground. This would help protect the personnel form such potential hazards as meteorite strikes, lethal radiation, and extremes of

NASA's plans for a lunar installation.

temperature. Then, when this below-ground installation was of a sufficient scale and in full working order to allow for a permanent presence to be successfully maintained, it could be dramatically expanded in size and scope to include significant surface facilities.

More and more additions would be made to the initial constructions: landing-pads for shuttle-craft were envisaged, and launch sites for both manned and unmanned missions to some of the nearby planets were deemed possible. Eventually, what had begun as a compact military outpost resembling those at the North and South Pole might conceivably mutate into a huge strategic facility acting as a major hub for both scientific studies and military operations deemed vital to the national security and technological advancement of the United States.

Whereas the U.S. Army of 1959 was secretly sure it could have a permanently manned installation ready to go at some point between 1965 and 1966, history has shown that it took pretty much all of NASA's time and expertise to even land a small team of men on the Moon by 1969. At the time, a Moon base was not in the cards for NASA. Some might suggest the military was being somewhat over-ambitious in its plans. For example, history has shown that, officially at least, Project Horizon was ultimately shelved as a result of budgetary concerns and the limitations of current technologies. Unofficially, some believe, Project Horizon—and perhaps further, far more ambitious programs—secretly continued, and ultimately led to the construction of large Top Secret installations on the Moon, not unlike that described by Karl Wolfe.

NASA and Gary McKinnon

Certain of NASA's publicly acknowledged programs have been the subject of intense secrecy: Between 1982 and 1992 the space agency's Space Shuttle fleet launched 11 classified payloads—spy satellites, in other words—for the U.S. intelligence community, particularly so for the super-secret National Reconnaissance Office. This we know. But far more notable is the strange saga of a certain Gary McKinnon. A product of the 1960s, and a man with a profound fascination for UFOs, McKinnon currently lives in London, England, under the dark shadow of extradition to the United States on charges of committing what one U.S. prosecutor has asserted was without doubt the largest computer hack of the United States's official infrastructure ever. The prosecution also alleges that McKinnon caused major damage to a whole host of NASA computers in the process, as a result of his obsession with UFOs.

I have written about McKinnon's antics at length in some of my other books, but what is especially relevant to this chapter is that McKinnon said he found files referencing something termed *Non-Terrestrial Officers*. This has led some commentators to speculate that it may be a reference to a secret team of American astronauts who are a part of an equally secret space program.

Richard Dolan

Another individual who has commented positively on issues relative to secret bases on the Moon and the theory that the U.S. government operates a clandestine space program is the respected author and historian Richard Dolan, who says, "Over the years I have encountered no shortage of quiet, serious-minded people who tell me of their knowledge that there is such a covert program. Are there bases on the far side of the Moon? I do not know for sure, but I cannot rule it out."[2]

Spy Satellites

And then there were the illuminating, albeit cryptic remarks of U.S. Senators Jay Rockefeller and Ron Wyden in December 2004. During a somewhat heated debate on the issue of the 2005 Intelligence Authorization Bill, they commented on their knowledge of the United States's covert space operations; a classified program that

Rockefeller described as being massively costly. He also noted, intriguingly, that attempts to kill the project (at least twice by the Senate) were always officially over-ruled. Steven Aftergood, of the Federation of American Scientists, suggested that the senators were talking, in couched terms, about a highly secret spy-satellite project.

The Men who stare at the Moon

We now come to the fascinating and undeniably unique saga of a man named Ingo Swann, who, in the 1970s, worked on the U.S. government's remote viewing program, which addressed the possibility of harnessing psychic powers and extrasensory perception (ESP) to spy on the former Soviet Union. Swann proved to be a highly skilled remote viewer, and his talents were employed on a number of espionage operations focusing on overseas targets that might have proven hostile to the United States. As a result, Swann came into contact with a variety of shadowy figures in the world of intelligence-gathering, including a truly Machiavellian character known, very mysteriously, only by the name of Mr. Axelrod.

It was in February 1975 that Swann was contacted out of the blue by a man he described as a highly placed figure in Washington, D.C., who guardedly advised Swann that he, Swann, would soon be receiving a telephone call from Mr. Axelrod. Swann's source quietly advised him that although he could not offer much of a meaningful explanation at that time, Swann should be keenly aware that the call would concern a matter of great urgency and importance. A somewhat concerned Swann waited. And waited...and waited.

Finally, around four weeks later, a call arrived, and Swann was asked to make a cloak-and-dagger rendezvous, mere hours later, at the Museum of Natural History at the Smithsonian (a location we have seen linked with the mystery and controversy surrounding.the reputed remains of Noah's Ark). Swann unhesitatingly agreed, and quickly—albeit with a degree of concern and trepidation—made his careful way to the meeting place, where he was greeted by a man whom Swann said looked like a Marine.

Basic formalities were exchanged, but Swann was hardly clear on what was afoot. He was driven by car to a second location, where a helicopter was waiting to take him to a destination unknown. Such was the security and secrecy surrounding the journey that Swann was blindfolded for the approximately 30-minute flight. On landing, Swann was taken to an elevator that descended for a significant period of time—perhaps into the bowels of some secret, underground installation, Swann thought. When the blindfold was finally removed, Swann was introduced to the enigmatic Mr. Axelrod, who admitted that it was not his real name, but one that served the particular purposes of their meeting.

Axelrod got straight to the point, asking Swann a great deal of questions about the nature of remote viewing. He also made it clear that he wished to make use of Swann's skills—on what was clearly a secret operation—for a significant sum of money. It truly was one of those offers that one cannot refuse. And Swann, most assuredly, did not refuse it.

Axelrod asked Swann, pointedly, what he knew about our Moon. Now, finally, the purpose of the strange meeting was becoming much clearer: Someone within officialdom was secretly looking to have the Moon re-mote-viewed. This is precisely what Swann went ahead and did. By his own admission, he was utterly floored by what he found: During an initial targeting, his mind focused in on sensational imagery that looked to be a huge tower, similar in size to the Secretariat Building at the United Nations, but one that soared upwards from the Moon's surface. This was no human-made structure, Swann was told; it was the work of nothing less than mysterious extraterrestrials.

In follow-up remote-viewing sessions, Swann was able to perceive on the surface of the Moon a wealth of domed structures, advanced machinery, additional tall towers, large cross-like structures, curious tubular con-structions across the landscape, and even evidence of what looked like extensive mining operations. Someone, or something, had secretly constructed a fully functioning Moon-base.

Swann was also able to focus his mind on what ap-peared to be a group of people—who appeared very human—housed in some sort of enclosure on the Moon, who were busily burrowing into the side of a cliff. The odd thing was that they were all completely naked. At that point Axelrod very quickly terminated the experi-ment, amid disturbing allusions to the possibility that the Moon-based entities were possibly aware that they were being spied upon via astral travel. It was even implied that Swann's actions might place him in grave danger, if the beings decided to turn the tables and pay him a deadly visit. (Fortunately for Swann, they did not.)

Axelrod also inquired of Swann whether he knew of a man named George Leonard. Swann replied that he was not familiar with the name. So who was George Leonard? During the same time frame that the shadowy Mr. Axelrod was employing Swann to seek out the mysteries of the Moon, Leonard, an author, was hard at work on a manuscript titled *Somebody Else is on the Moon*. Leonard's manuscript was published in 1977, and focused on the very matter about which Axelrod was so deeply troubled: unusual, intelligently designed structures, or installations, on the Moon. The odd meetings between Swann and Axelrod—on the nature of what was afoot on the Moon—continued until 1977, after which they came to an abrupt end, with Swann left scratching his head.

Had Swann *really* psychically accessed a fantastically advanced base on the Moon that had been constructed by space-faring extraterrestrials? Or does the fact that Swann saw beings that looked like people—albeit naked ones!—working at the base mean that this secret installation had very terrestrial origins, which Axelrod was trying to learn more about because he was left out of the highly classified loop? If the former scenario is correct, then Swann's discoveries are profound in the extreme. If the latter theory has merit, however, it might very well be argued that the U.S. Army's secret 1960s operation to build a base on the Moon (under the auspices of Project Horizon) was not quite as cancelled as the military wished us to believe.

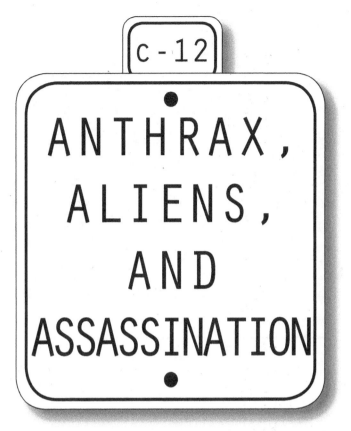

ANTHRAX, ALIENS, AND ASSASSINATION

PORTON DOWN IS ONE OF THE MOST secretive of all government installations in the United Kingdom. It can be found in the green and pleasant county of Wiltshire, and its classified work focuses on exotic viruses and biological-warfare. Although the secret work at Porton Down originally began at the height of the tumultuous First World War, it was not until the dawning of the 1940s that the installation became the central hub for British interest in the expanding realms of chemical and biological warfare. From 1946 onward, one year after the successful defeat of Nazi Germany, Porton Down's work began to focus more on the defensive—rather than chiefly offensive—uses of such warfare, and in 1957

179

Porton Down: bio-warfare central.

the installation was duly christened the Microbiological Research Establishment.

By the late 1970s, a decision was made to place the MRE under the control of a civil body. As a result, there was a significant reorganization, and on April 1, 1979, the Microbiological Research Establishment became the Center for Applied Microbiology and Research. Then, in 1995, it was absorbed into the Defense Evaluation and Research Agency (DERA). Six years later, there was yet another change: DERA split into two organizations, a private body called QinetiQ, and the Defense Science and Technology Laboratory, an arm of the Ministry of Defense steeped in official secrecy. Today, the facility is known as DSTL, Porton Down.

Although Porton Down has been careful to cultivate and maintain its image as a facility whose work is purely defensive in nature and relatively open to parliamentary scrutiny and official oversight, in reality this is far from the case. Porton Down is not without its dark side. During the 1950s, for example, a select number of British military personnel were—unbeknownst to them—given LSD at Porton Down as part of a classified effort to determine the effects of the drug and ascertain the extent to which it might have a viable role to play in warfare, perhaps by rendering enemy personnel incapable of engaging in hostilities.

Furthermore, at least as far back as the early 1950s, Porton Down was also secretly exposing military personnel to nerve gas, again to try and understand its potential role in warfare. Sometimes, this action proved to be recklessly and tragically costly: In 1953, Ron Maddison, a 20-year-old serviceman with the British Royal Air Force, died after Porton Down scientists ruthlessly exposed him to Sarin, an extremely toxic chemical agent that is now classed as a Weapon of Mass Destruction under the United Nations Security Council Resolution 687, which came into being in April 1991.

Top secret work at Porton Down

It is intriguing to note that, in addition to its regular (albeit controversial and Top Secret) work here described, Porton Down has been directly linked to two additional highly controversial issues:

1. UFOs and alien life.
2. A series of mysterious deaths that dominated the elite field of microbiology in the first decade of the 21st century.

Let us start with the former.

UFOs and Alien Life

On the night of January 23, 1974, an enigmatic event occurred in the large Berwyn Mountain range in North Wales, United Kingdom, that, for some within the UFO research community, has come to be known as the British Roswell. Researcher Andy Roberts summed up this mysterious affair: "The claim was that a UFO piloted by extraterrestrials crashed, or was shot down, on the mountain known as Cader Berwyn and that the alien crew, some still alive, were whisked off to a secret military installation in the south of England for study."[1]

That secret military installation was said to be none other than Porton Down. Of course, this sounds like a conspiracy theorist's wildest dream come true, but despite vociferous attacks from the more skeptical members of the UFO research community, it has steadfastly remained an integral part of the story ever since it first surfaced (publicly, at least) in 1996. The original source of this Porton Down story was a now-deceased UFO investigator named Tony Dodd, a North Yorkshire, England police sergeant with a quarter of a century of service on the Force. At the time the account was first revealed, Dodd flatly refused to reveal to *anyone* the real name of the source for his sensational story, and instead preferred to provide the pseudonym of James Prescott.

According to "Prescott," at the time of the Berwyn incident he was stationed at an Army barracks in the south of England. Stressing to Dodd that he could not name either his unit or his barracks, as they were still very much operational, Prescott said that by January 18, 1974, it was clear that something unusual was afoot: He and his colleagues were placed on emergency stand-by status. The reason why became apparent 24 hours later, when Prescott's unit was directed to make its way carefully and quietly toward the English city of Birmingham.

The team then received orders to proceed with speed towards North Wales, but were halted on the outskirts of the English city of Chester, in readiness for a military exercise they were told was about to take place in the area. Not long after, the orders changed yet again, and they were to make their way to the town of Llangollen, in northeast Wales. On arrival at Llangollen, recalled Prescott, the unit noticed a great deal of ground activity in the area. In addition, military aircraft were soaring across the darkened Welsh skies. Extraordinary events were clearly unfolding at an extremely fast rate. It was shortly after 11:30 p.m. when the situation began to take shape, and Prescott and his colleagues were on the move once more: to the village of Llandderfel. The team soon reached the little hamlet, whereupon they were directed to load two large, oblong boxes into their vehicle: "We were at this time warned not to open the boxes, but to proceed to Porton Down and deliver the boxes."[2]

A number of hours later, they reached the secret Wiltshire facility and were duly directed to a specific part of the installation. Once inside, explained Prescott, the boxes were opened by staff at the facility in their presence. He could see that they contained two strange, unearthly creatures that had been placed inside decontamination suits. The staff at Porton then began the careful task of opening the suits. Prescott said that when this action was complete it was clear to all those present that the entities were not of this Earth. He elaborated: "What I saw in the boxes that day made me change my whole concept of life. The bodies were about five to six feet tall, humanoid in shape, but so thin they looked almost skeletal with a covering skin. Although I did not see a craft at the scene of the recovery, I was informed that a large craft had crashed and was recovered by other military units."[3]

Perhaps even more remarkable was what Prescott had to say next: Shortly after his life-changing experience at Porton Down, he had the opportunity to speak with several colleagues from his own unit, who guardedly informed him they had also transported aliens to Porton Down, but with one amazing difference. *"Their cargo was still alive."*[4]

And that's where the Berwyn Mountains story dries up, unfortunately. But the Porton Down/UFO link continues.

Invasion Earth

As I noted in a previous chapter of this book, Nick Pope, who officially investigated UFO reports for the British Ministry of Defense from 1991 to 1994, wrote a novel in 1999 titled *Operation Thunder Child* that focused upon a hostile attack on the British Isles by alien entities. In the book, alien bodies recovered from a UFO crash are secretly taken to Porton Down.

At the same time that Nick Pope was writing his book, the British Ministry of Defense, in a truly unprecedented move, gave a huge amount of technical assistance and support to a BBC science-fiction production titled

Invasion Earth that dealt with an attack on the planet by hostile alien entities. Inevitably, rumors began that this move was a less-than-subtle attempt by certain elements of the British government to get the general public thinking about the possibility of waging war against an alien species. Did the MoD know something that the rest of us didn't? A Ministry of Defense source—who was *specifically* referred to me directly by Nick Pope—had a number of perceptive comments to make on this particularly odd set of circumstances: "It's extremely strange," said the man, "that on the one hand the MoD is publicly so dismissive about UFOs, and yet on the other they bent over backwards to provide assistance to a TV company producing a science-fiction drama which starts with the Royal Air Force shooting down a UFO. Normally, the Ministry of Defense only helps film and TV companies where it believes that significant benefits will fall to the MoD in terms of recruiting, training, or public relations. This was the case, for example, with our participation in the James Bond film, *Tomorrow Never Dies*. What, one wonders, did the MoD think it had to gain from helping to perpetuate a view that the Royal Air Force were virtually at war with extraterrestrials? Questions about our participation in this project were raised at the highest level within the Ministry of Defense."[5]

Most notable of all, in *Invasion Earth*, a number of aliens retrieved from a crashed and captured UFO are taken to—yes—Porton Down.

UFOs at Rendlesham Forest

There is one final footnote to the Porton Down UFO controversy: the famous UFO incident at Rendlesham Forest, Suffolk, England in December 1980. The event has been the subject of half a dozen books, and is considered by many to be a prime example of a UFO landing. The basics of the account are these: Between December 26 and 29, 1980, multiple UFO encounters occurred within Rendlesham Forest, and involved United States military personnel based at the nearby Royal Air Force stations Bentwaters and Woodbridge. According to numerous U.S. Air Force personnel, a small, triangular shaped object was seen maneuvering in the forest. Others, such as the previously mentioned Larry Warren, told of traumatic encounters deep within the trees, with strange, spectral, alien-style entities.

Less well known is the fact that the late Rendlesham researcher and author Georgina Bruni uncovered a rumor suggesting that shortly after the events in the forest occurred, a number of personnel from Porton Down were covertly dispatched to the area. Significantly, the Porton Down team was dressed in full-body protection suits—or Hazmat outfits, as they have become known—and tentatively entered the woods, for reasons that remain unknown outside of official channels.

On January 11, 2001, the late British Admiral of the Fleet, Lord Hill-Norton, who had a personal interest in UFOs in general and the Rendlesham affair in particular, asked questions at an official level with British authorities in an attempt to resolve the issue of the Porton Down allegations as they related to the Rendlesham case. Predictably, the response to Hill-Norton's questions, which surfaced on January 25, 2001, was that staff at Porton Down had made careful checks of their archives, but had found no record of any such visit to the woods. It should be noted this did not mean such records did not exist, only that the specific personnel who made the search were unable to locate anything of relevance. The controversy surrounding crashed UFOs, biological warfare, and Porton Down seemed destined to continue.

Deaths in Microbiology

From the latter part of 2001 to the present day, literally dozens of individuals working within the elite field of microbiology (the study of organisms that are too small to be seen with the naked eye, such as bacteria and viruses, some of which are lethal) in various countries around the world have died under suspicious circumstances. Many of the deaths appear, at first glance at least, to have prosaic explanations: suicides, illnesses, and accidents. There are those, however, who have maintained that the sheer number of such deaths cannot be explained away so easily. More intriguing is the fact that many of the now-dead microbiologists had links to worldwide intelligence services, including the United States's CIA, Britain's MI5 and MI6, and Israel's Mossad.

Inevitably, this strange cluster of deaths in such a tightly knit area of cutting-edge research has led to a proliferation of conspiracy theories. Some students of the puzzle believe that a cell of deep-cover terrorists from the Middle East is attempting to wipe out the leading names within the field of microbiology as part of an ongoing plot to prevent Western nations from developing the ultimate bio-weapon. A much darker and controversial theory suggests that this same weapon has *already* been developed, and now, with their work complete, the micro-biologists are being systematically killed off by elements of Western Intelligence, in an effort to prevent them being kidnapped by terrorists who will then force them to work for the other side. Of particular relevance to this chapter is the fact that a number of those same scientists had ties—some very significant ties—to Porton Down.

On November 23, 2001, Dr. Vladimir Pasechnik, a former microbiologist for Bioreparat—a bio-weapons production facility that existed in Russia prior to the collapse of the Soviet Union—was found dead near his home in the county of Wiltshire, England—the very county that just happens to be home to Porton Down. Pasechnik's defection to Britain in 1989 revealed to Western intelligence services, for the very first time, the sheer extent and scale of the former Soviet Union's secret research into the field of biological warfare, including deadly anthrax. After his defection, Pasechnik was employed for a year at the Center for Applied Microbiology Research at Porton Down before forming his own company, called Regma Biotechnics. In the final weeks of his life, Pasechnik placed the sum total of his anthrax-based research in the hands of the British government. According to British Intelligence, Pasechnik died of nothing stranger than a tragic stroke. How very convenient that Pasechnik's fatal stroke did not hit him until precisely *after* he had completed his work on Anthrax and handed it over to British authorities.

Then, on July 18, 2003, David Kelly, a British biological-weaponry expert, fatally slashed his own wrists while out walking in woods near his home. At least, that was the official version of events. Kelly was the British Ministry of Defense's Chief Scientific Officer and Senior Adviser to the Proliferation and Arms Control Secretariat, and to the Foreign Office's non-proliferation department. In 1984, Kelly had been appointed as Head of Microbiology at Porton Down. In the autumn of 1989, he was called in to assist MI6 in debriefing none other than the aforementioned Vladimir Pasechnik. This debriefing provided undeniable evidence of a gross violation of the 1972 biological weapons convention: the Russians were shown to be secretly studying the Smallpox virus, in direct, flagrant contravention of World Health Organization regulations. After the Iraqis were slung out of Kuwait in 1991, the U.N. invited Kelly to help force Saddam Hussein into compliance with the peace agreements. Kelly made 36 visits to Iraq, and, from New York, continued his work into the late 1990s. He also acted as the Senior Adviser on Biological Weapons to the United Nations' Biological Weapons Inspections teams (Unscom) from 1994 to 1999. To this day, Kelly's suicide is viewed with deep suspicion and great cynicism.

On July 3, 2004, nearly a year after Kelly's passing, 52-year-old Dr. Paul Norman of Salisbury, Wiltshire, England, was killed when the Cessna 206 aircraft he was piloting crashed in the English county of Devonshire. Dr. Norman was the Chief Scientist for Chemical and Biological Defense at Porton Down. The Cessna's crash site was sealed off, and was examined by officials from the Air Accidents Investigation Branch. The wreckage of the aircraft was removed from the site to the AAIB's base of operations at Farnborough, England. The crash, as no one should be surprised to learn, was ruled an accident. Uh-huh.

Were the deaths of Pasechnik, Kelly, and Norman really so prosaic, as the British Government was—and still very much is—so keen to assert? Or was the fact that all three had secret ties to Porton Down an indication that something stranger and far more deadly was afoot? In today's climate of terror, it should be recognized that *any* suspicious deaths in the field of microbiology and biological warfare—specifically where the victims had links to the Intelligence services of a number of countries and secret installations like Porton Down—might be an indication that a terrorist assassination squad was at work.

$$\bigcirc$$

Now let's focus our attention upon the United States's equivalent of Porton Down: Fort Detrick.

Fort Detrick

In 1941, President Roosevelt secretly ordered the establishment of a program that came to be officially known as the U.S. Biological Warfare Program. As a result of Roosevelt's historic move, in 1943, the newly designated Camp Detrick, in Maryland, was assigned to the Army Chemical Warfare Service for the specific development of a center dedicated to biological warfare issues. Twelve months later, Camp Detrick was established as an installation focused on the research and development of both offensive and defensive biological warfare techniques and agents.

In 1956, the name of the installation was changed from Camp Detrick to Fort Detrick, but its workload remained very much the same. Then, on April 1, 1972, following the official closure of offensive biological warfare studies in the United States, the control of Fort Detrick was transferred from the U.S. Army Material Command to the Office of the Surgeon General, Department of the Army. One year later, Fort Detrick was assigned to the newly created U.S. Army Health Services Command. And in 1995, the HSC was itself reorganized, into the U.S. Army Medical Command. Perhaps not surprisingly, Fort Detrick, just like Porton Down, is a hotbed of controversial deaths.

Few people who lived through it will ever likely forget the incredible wave of terror that swept the United States when, only one week after the shocking events of September 11, 2001 unfolded, anonymously mailed envelopes containing anthrax spores arrived at the offices of a variety of major media outlets, including the *New York Post*, *CBS News*, and *ABC News*. Two Democratic senators, Tom Daschle and Patrick Leahy, were also targeted with the potentially deadly substance. The results were catastrophic. At least 22 people were infected, of whom five tragically lost their lives. The situation led the FBI to launch one of the biggest manhunts in its long and winding history.

Documentation that has surfaced via the provisions of the Freedom of Information Act shows that, by the early months of 2005, the FBI had a suspect in the anthrax mailings case firmly in mind. It was not some minion of Osama Bin Laden or Saddam Hussein, however, as many had assumed (and as many within the administration

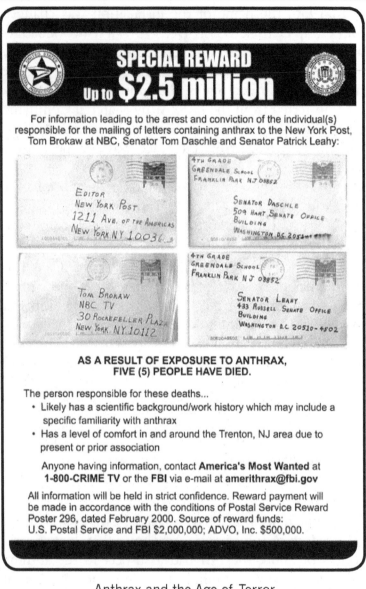

Anthrax and the Age of Terror.

of George W. Bush earnestly hoped would be the case). Rather, it was a Dr. Bruce Edwards Ivins, a microbiologist who had worked for the United States Army Medical Research Institute of Infectious Diseases (USAMRIID) at Fort Detrick for no less than 18 years.

By 2007, Ivins became the subject of periodic secret surveillance by the FBI personnel assigned to the operation. And it did not take the FBI long to build up what was perceived by the Bureau as a very strong case against the man: In June 2008, Ivins was informed that prosecution for the anthrax attacks, as well as for the subsequent injuries and deaths, was almost certainly forthcoming. Ivins did not wait around to learn what the FBI had in store for him. On July 27, 2008, he died as a result of a significant overdose of acetaminophen, a pain reliever. As was the case with the various microbiologists attached to Porton Down, England, whose lives ended so abruptly and suspiciously in this very same time frame, probing questions were asked as to whether Ivins had really taken his own life, or if he was merely a convenient scapegoat for a far bigger, wide-ranging conspiracy.

One theory suggested that Ivins was nothing more than a Lee Harvey Oswald–style patsy, and that the anthrax attacks were actually the work of rogue elements within the Bush Administration that were intent on terrorizing the nation to such a degree that no one would even dare to question Dubya's plans to invade the Middle East and establish footholds in both Iraq and Afghanistan before then moving on to Iran, and who knew where else after that.

FBI sources stated that in the direct aftermath of the anthrax attacks, the White House practically *ordered*

Robert Mueller, director of the FBI, to find a link—*any* link, no matter how tenuous—between the anthrax attacker and Osama bin Laden. Despite the unrelenting pressure put on Mueller, FBI agents wryly noted that there was no way whatsoever that the particular strain of anthrax in question could have been fashioned by "some guy in a cave."[6]

Whether or not the FBI was right to focus on Ivins, Dr. Meryl Nass, an authority on anthrax, said that regardless of how accurate microbial forensics might be, that discipline would only have the ability to connect the anthrax to a specific strain and place of origin, and not to any particular individual. Regardless, as a result of the fact that Ivins was now dead and the FBI had no other target in sight, it elected to close its investigation on February 19, 2010. Not everyone was satisfied with the outcome, however.

Echoing the sentiments of many, Senator Leahy—who had been one of the key targets of the anthrax attacks—said of the theory that Ivins had been the sole culprit, "If he is the one who sent the letter, I do not believe in any way, shape, or manner that he is the only person involved in this attack on Congress and the American people. I do not believe that at all."[7]

There is a curious afterword to this story: Militarized Anthrax, as it is known, was developed by William C. Patrick III, who, throughout the course of an extensive, multifaceted career, was employed at Fort Detrick and the equally secret Dugway Proving Grounds in Utah, and periodically undertook contract work for the CIA. Patrick, who died in 2010 at the age of 84, developed a process by which anthrax spores could be concentrated at a level of one trillion spores per gram, which happens to be the precise concentration of the anthrax utilized in the 2001 attacks—yet another clear indicator that, regardless of the role played (or not played) by Ivins, the anthrax attacks were domestic in origin. Aside from the United States, no nation on the planet has ever successfully managed to achieve concentrations above 500 billion per gram.

In later years Patrick worked closely with a certain Colonel Kanatjan Alibekov, who rose through the ranks of the Soviet Army to become the first Deputy Director of the Russian equivalent of Fort Detrick and Porton Down: Biopreparat. Alibekov, who defected to the United States in 1992, now goes by the far more Western moniker of Ken Alibek. Interestingly (some might say highly curiously), before his defection, Alibekov's boss was none other than Dr. Vladimir Pasechnik, who, as we have seen, was an expert in the field of anthrax research, and died under questionable circumstances in Wiltshire, England, in November 2001, only a month after the anthrax attacks in the United States were at their height.

Whether as a result of its reported ties to anthrax attacks, the Age of Terror, and groundbreaking research into the realm of biological warfare, Fort Detrick, just like its British cousin, Porton Down, remains an enigmatic installation.

C - 13

THE SECRET ISLAND

THE COMMONWEALTH OF PUERTO RICO IS WHAT is known as an unincorporated territory of the United States, and is located in the Caribbean Sea. According to some, it may very well be the most secrecy-shrouded place on the planet, home to not just one secret base, but a plethora of classified locations, certainly of a governmental nature, and maybe even of an alien nature too. Throughout the course of the last 20 years or so, the people of Puerto Rico have been swamped by UFO encounters, sightings of strange and unearthly craft surfacing from mountainous lairs and undersea installations, and run-ins with strange, vampiric creatures that one might accurately describe as the distinctly evil twins of Steven Spielberg's benign E.T.

A secret installation is said to exist in these
coastal waters off Puerto Rico.

For two decades, controversial tales have surfaced from
Puerto Rico describing a killer beast creeping around the
landscape, plunging the population into a state of fear
and apprehension. The face of this monster is dominated
by a pair of glowing red eyes; it has razor-sharp, claw-
like appendages, vicious-looking teeth that could likely
inflict some truly serious damage, sharp spikes running
down its neck and spine, and even, on occasion, large
membranous wings. On top of that, the creature thrives
on blood. Puerto Rico, then, is home to a real-life vampire. Its moniker is the Chupacabra, a Latin term meaning "goat-sucker"—in reference to the fact that when the
Chupacabra tales first surfaced in the 1990s, most of the
animals slain by the blood-sucking nightmare were goats.
That's right: If you're a goat, it most certainly does not
pay to make Puerto Rico your home. It might not be too
safe if you're human either.

Theories abound with respect to the nature of the beast. Some researchers and witnesses suggest that the monster is some form of giant bat; others prefer the theory that it has extraterrestrial origins. Certainly the most bizarre idea postulated is that the Chupacabra is the creation of a Top Secret genetic research laboratory hidden deep within Puerto Rico's El Yunque rainforest, in the Sierra de Luquillo, approximately 25 miles southeast of the city of San Juan.

El Yunque was named after the Indian spirit Yuquiyu, but is also known as the Caribbean National Forest, and is the only rainforest in the U.S. National Forest System. Its 28,000 acres are a glorious sight to behold: More than 100 billion gallons of precipitation fall each year, creating the jungle-like ambience of lush foliage, sparkling leaves, spectacular waterfalls, shining wet rocks, and shadowy paths that really have to be seen up close and personal to be appreciated. The forest contains rare wildlife as well, including the Puerto Rican Parrot, the Puerto Rican Boa snake, a multitude of lizards and crabs, and of course the famous Coquí frog, so named after its unique vocalizations.

As for the Chupacabra...well, its predations and appearance are as legendary as they are feared. Although I could cite case after case, nearly ad infinitum, for our purposes one will suffice.

Norka's Chupacabra

Norka is an elderly lady living in a truly beautiful home high in the El Yunque rainforest that one can only reach by negotiating an infinitely complex series of treacherous roads, built perilously close to the edge of some very steep hills. Although the exact date escapes her, Norka remembers driving home one night in 1975 or 1976, when she was both startled and horrified by the sight of a bizarre creature shambling across the road.

She described the animal as approximately four feet in height, with a monkey-like body that was covered in dark brown hair or fur, wings that were a cross between those of a bat and those of a bird, and glowing eyes that bulged alarmingly from a bat-like visage. Sharp claws flicked ominously in Norka's direction. She could only sit and stare as the beast then turned its back on her and rose slowly into the sky. Since then, eerily similar encounters with such vile entities have haunted the terrified populace of Puerto Rico. They may have also attracted the attention of the official world too.

The El Yunque Rainforest: the lair of the Chupacabra.

Roosevelt Roads

On one of my several expeditions to Puerto Rico, a number of residents suggested it would be a very good idea for me to focus my attention upon the links between the beast and a former U.S. Naval base called Roosevelt Roads, located in the town of Ceiba. Today the site holds the José Aponte de la Torre Airport, but in 1944, when the base was inaugurated, it was perceived as a place of prime strategic importance—particularly so if the island became the site of hostilities with unfriendly nations. By 1957, Roosevelt Roads had been officially designated as a Naval Station. To demonstrate its importance from a military perspective, the U.S. Naval Forces Southern Command (USNAVSO) had its base of operations at Roosevelt Roads. In January 2004, however, the Navy elected to relocate USNAVSO to Naval Station Mayport, Florida. When the Navy finally moved out of the base on March 31, 2004, it was seen as a victory for those on the island seeking independence.

But what about the link between Roosevelt Roads and the Chupacabra? According to the stories that were coming from all across Puerto Rico, a number of captured, very vicious Chupacabra had supposedly been briefly held within a secure, secret facility at Roosevelt Roads at some point in the early 1990s, before being secretly shipped to the States (probably to Area 51, or to some similar desert locale). This same story, in various incarnations and to varying degrees, was told to me by numerous individuals on the island. I was also informed that stories had been quietly circulating among the island's inhabitants for years to the effect that there were some distinctly strange things going on deep in the rainforest at what was described to me as a "secret monkey research center." So the rumors went, biological warfare tests, genetic manipulation, and even more horrifying experimentation were the order of the day there, and some of the unfortunate animals that had been experimented on were said to have escaped from their confines and run wild on the island. At least a few of those animals, it was suspected by locals on the island, could have been responsible for the tales of the exploits of the Chupacabra.

The caribbean primate Research center

Accounts such as these, suggesting the Chupacabra was the result of gene-splicing experimentation by crazed scientists, proliferated. Notably, the CIA was also linked with this theoretical research center, and it was said that its interest was focused specifically upon social behavior studies related to monkey experimentation and Chupacabra attacks. However, it's highly unlikely that even the very best scientists on the payroll of the United States government possess the skills to successfully mutate a friendly little monkey into a rampaging, blood-sucking killing machine with glowing eyes, razor-sharp claws, and spikes running down the length of its back. And yet there is no doubt that intriguing things of a genetic nature have occurred deep in the forest.

Furthermore, such a primate facility most assuredly does exist.

Created in 1938, it was (and still is) called the Caribbean Primate Research Center (CPRC), and it is a research, training, and education unit of the University of Puerto Rico, which attracts the attention of the U.S. government and receives funding and support from the National Institutes of Health and the National Center for Research Resources. In the words of the CPRC itself, its mission revolves around "the study and use of non-human primates [chiefly, Indian rhesus monkeys] as models for studies of social and biological interactions and for the discovery of methods of prevention, diagnosis, and treatment of diseases that afflict humans."[1]

The Virology Laboratory of the CPRC is at the forefront of research to develop and simulate vaccines against SIV—or, as it is known in simpler terms, Monkey AIDS. It was this laboratory about which the locals had a great deal to say. And they weren't afraid to say it either. This was the scenario: A number of monkeys had escaped from the center some years earlier, and were now wildly running riot and breeding in the dense woods. Most disturbing was the fact that the original escapees were those that had contracted SIV and were being used in experiments to try and find a cure for HIV—experiments that were, notably, of intense interest to certain elements of the U.S. government. In other words, infected monkeys were on the loose in Puerto Rico.

It was highly possible, I was informed, that some attacks attributed to Puerto Rico's most famous vampire were really the result of the predations of very aggressive, SIV-infected monkeys. Arguably, that would be a very good reason for the U.S. government to create and circulate spurious tales about the Chupacabra: The story would act as very good camouflage in the event of any truly horrific attacks on local livestock, or, worse still, on people. As a bonus, the tales suggesting a Chupacabra presence in the area would hopefully ensure that the terrified locals kept their distance. On all of these thorny issues, the Caribbean Primate Research Center offers nothing more than an intriguing silence.

$$\bigcirc$$

With the Chupacabra mystery, and its links to both the U.S. Navy presence at Roosevelt Roads and the Caribbean Primate Research Center now detailed, let us focus on the other big mystery that dominates Puerto Rico: that of unidentified aerial craft. As with the saga of the Chupacabra, one could wax lyrically for countless pages on the many and varied UFO reports that have emanated from Puerto Rico since the late 1990s.

Rosario's Sighting

Rosario is a middle-aged woman living in the old San Juan district of Puerto Rico who earns her living in the island's food industry. In March 2000, she was working in a grove near the foot of the El Yunque rainforest. As she picked plantains (a type of fruit similar to a banana) her attention was drawn to a deep, resonating hum that seemed to come from directly above her. Looking up, Rosario was startled to see a black, triangular-shaped object, about 35 feet in length and with a shiny coating, hovering overhead at a height estimated to be around 90 to 120 feet.

Surprise and amazement turned to horror and shock when a pencil-thin beam of light shot out of the bottom of the object. The light-beam fanned out and enveloped Rosario in a pink glow. For what seemed like an eternity—but what was, Rosario says now, certainly less than a minute—she was rooted to the spot, while her mind was flooded with stark imagery of widespread nuclear destruction and environmental collapse in the Earth's near future. The final image was that of a large, bald head with huge black eyes staring at her—a definitive alien entity, in other words, of the type that has become infamous in today's world. Suddenly, the UFO soared upwards and headed slowly towards the thick rainforest. In the wake of the encounter, Rosario developed an overwhelming interest in environmental issues, and, quite literally overnight, after a lifetime of eating meat, became a staunch advocate of vegetarianism.

Alien Bases

Given the sheer scale of the UFO activity and Chupacabra encounters on Puerto Rico, this matter has inevitably given rise to a widely supported theory among the populace that the island is home to an underground or undersea base of extraterrestrial origins. Certainly, stories abound of UFOs seen entering and leaving secret alien bases across and around Puerto Rico. For example, Carlos Manuel Mercado maintains that in June 1988 he was taken to one such base, located in the Sierra Bermeja, which is adjacent to Puerto Rico's Laguna Cartagena National Wildlife Refuge. (Interestingly, the refuge falls under the jurisdiction of none other than the U.S. government's Fish and Wildlife Service, whose 2009 recommendations to restrict public access to large portions of the cave system are discussed in another chapter of this book in the context of the 2012 controversy.)

According to Mercado, he was taken to a huge, futuristic, factory-like alien installation buried deep inside a mountain known as El Cayul, where row after row of aliens were hard at work building and repairing a multitude of extraterrestrial spacecraft. The aliens, Mercado said, encouraged him to spread his story of encountering them in their secret installation far and wide, after his return to civilization.

In a similar vein, the UFO researcher Timothy Good, who personally interviewed Mercado in 1997, spoke with a Puerto Rican investigator of both the UFO and the Chupacabra phenomena named Jorge Martin, who advised Good that he, Martin, had received confirmation of the existence of the alien base within El Cayul from a high-ranking military officer.

Of course, stories like this are bound to provoke deep controversy. But it might be argued that everything about Puerto Rico's many mysteries and cosmic wonders provokes controversy, so why should the story of this apparently secret, mountainous facility be any different? So much for the base within El Cayul. But what about those rumors of undersea installations of a distinctly nonhuman nature?

Much of the evidence (which is admittedly fragmentary) points to the island of Vieques, a 21-mile-long landmass located, interestingly enough, near to the old Roosevelt Roads U.S. Navy facility where, as I discussed earlier, a number of *very* bad-tempered Chupacabra were supposedly briefly held in the early 1990s. Jorge Martin has uncovered a wealth of data on sightings of strange-looking craft of unknown origin and intent, both entering and leaving the waters that surround the island. In one case, from 1996, Martin was told by the primary eyewitness—a fisherman out at sea—of a huge, brightly lit, saucer-shaped craft that rose out of the waters near the Playa Grande lagoon.

A similar report from the same location, involving the sighting of a huge, triangular-shaped, silver-colored UFO, was provided to Jonathan Downes and I in 2004 by a former civil-defense employee, who had seen the gigantic craft rise silently out of the coastal waters of the island while he was on an early morning jog in the spring of 1999. In this case, the vast device, which was viewed at a distance of around half a mile off the coast, wobbled slightly, rather like a falling leaf, as it took to the skies, and then streaked vertically at a fantastic speed, growing ever smaller until it was finally lost from view due to the effects of the bright, rising sun.

Further rumors were provided to Downes and me on that expedition: They came from a retired police officer who had heard rumors to the effect that, somewhere off the coast of Puerto Rico (he was not entirely sure where, exactly), in late 1993, elements of the U.S. Navy spent several days tracking, via sonar, the movements of a huge UFO in the deep waters off Puerto Rico. Perhaps aware of its potentially hazardous nature, the U.S. Navy contingent, Downes and I were told, was ordered to merely carefully log the movements of the undersea craft, but never to engage it any way that might be interpreted as hostile.

Ø

Taking all these accounts into thoughtful consideration, is it truly feasible that Puerto Rico might be home to a massive undersea installation? When one realizes that we, the human race, have had the ability to construct such futuristic facilities for decades, then the possibility becomes not so unbelievable after all. And make no mistake: Evidence of our own undersea abilities is far from lacking. For example, an October 1966 document prepared by C.F. Austin of the U.S. Naval Ordnance Test Station at China Lake, California, includes a truly remarkable statement. Titled "Manned Undersea Structures—The Rock-Site Concept," it states in part: "Large undersea installations with a shirt-sleeve environment have existed under the continental shelves for many decades. The technology now exists, using off-the-shelf petroleum, mining, submarine, and nuclear equipment, to establish permanent manned installations within the sea floor that do not have any air umbilical or other connection with the land or water surface, yet maintain a normal one-atmosphere environment within."[2]

If, as this previously classified U.S. Navy document demonstrates, the government of the United States was constructing undersea installations a number of decades before the documentation was even prepared in the mid-1960s, perhaps someone else, someone from a world far, far away, has secretly been doing likewise. And just maybe they chose Puerto Rico as their base of operations.

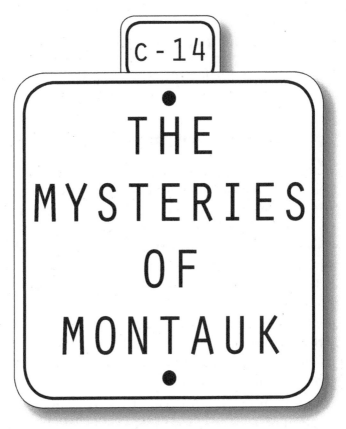

c - 14

THE MYSTERIES OF MONTAUK

CONSPIRACY THEORISTS ALLEGE THAT, AT a relatively innocuous-looking location on Long Island, New York—originally called Camp Hero, and later renamed the Montauk Air Force Station—highly classified research has, for decades, been undertaken into a dizzying array of far-out issues, including time travel, teleportation, invisibility, and mind control. Whether the tales are the absolute truth, overwhelming fiction, or a swirling, hazy combination of both, only one thing is certain: They absolutely refuse to roll over and die. In the more than two decades that have now passed since the controversial stories first surfaced, they have spawned a veritable industry, with books galore, lectures and conferences, television documentaries, and magazine articles all focused intently upon what has become known as the Montauk Project.

The Philadelphia Experiment

Before we get to the meat of what whole swathes of conspiracy-minded people are devoted to believing has been going on at the Montauk Air Force Station for years, we have to take a trip through time, back to the height of the Second World War, when strange and unearthly things were reportedly afoot in the heart of the Philadelphia Naval Yard. The bulk of the rumors and testimony suggests that the fantastic, Top Secret research allegedly undertaken at Montauk began as a direct outgrowth of an equally fantastic and highly classified project of the U.S. Navy. It has become infamously known as the Philadelphia Experiment.

The genesis of the story dates back to 1955, with the publication of *The Case for the UFO* by the late Morris K. Jessup, a book that delved deeply into two key issues:

1. The theoretical power source of UFOs.
2. The utilization of the universal gravitational field as a form of energy.

Not long after the publication of the book, Jessup became the recipient of a series of extremely strange missives from a certain Carlos Miquel Allende, of Pennsylvania. In his correspondence, Allende commented on Jessup's theories, and gave details of an alleged secret experiment conducted by the U.S. Navy in the Philadelphia Naval Yard in October 1943. According to Allende's incredible tale, during the experiment a warship was rendered

The Philadelphia Naval Shipyard: The
origin of the Montauk Project.

optically invisible and teleported to and from Norfolk,
Virginia, in a few minutes. The incredible feat was supposedly accomplished by applying Albert Einstein's never-
completed Unified Field theory.

Allende elaborated that the ship used in the experiment was the DE 173 USS *Eldridge*, and, moreover, that
he had actually witnessed one of the attempts to render
both the ship and its crew invisible from his position out
at sea onboard a steamer called the SS *Andrew Furuseth*.

From the safety of the *Furuseth*, Allende, in his own words, said he "watched the air all around the ship turn slightly, ever so slightly, darker than all the other air. I saw, after a few minutes, a foggy green mist arise like a cloud. I watched as thereafter the DE 173 became rapidly invisible to human eyes."[1]

If Allende was telling the truth, then the Navy had not only begun to grasp the nature of invisibility, but it had also stumbled upon the secret of teleportation. Allende claimed that the experiment rendered many of the crew-members as mad as hatters, and some even literally vanished from the ship while the test was at its height, never to be seen again—at least not in 1943. Others reportedly became fused into the metal hull of the ship itself, destined to die horrific and agonizing deaths.

It is a matter of official record that Carlos Allende *did* serve aboard the SS *Andrew Furuseth* during the time frame that he claimed to have witnessed the secret experiment. Crucial to the controversy surrounding the strange saga of the USS *Eldridge* is whether or not Allende was speaking truthfully, and if the case for the reality of the Philadelphia Experiment stands or falls on his words alone. The U.S. Navy's position on the Philadelphia Experiment is that Allende's story was completely bogus. But such was its allure, even the Navy admits, that it spawned a legend that just refuses to go away. However, despite the Navy's assertions that the entire controversy can be traced back to Allende and no one else, that is most assuredly not the case.

Philadelphia Experiment investigators Bill Moore and Charles Berlitz uncovered a clipping culled from a presently unidentified newspaper of the 1940s that appears to confirm one of the strangest aspects of Allende's account: namely, that some of the sailors who were onboard the *Eldridge* during the fateful experiment later vanished into thin air during a barroom brawl near the Philadelphia harbor.

Titled "Strange Circumstances Surround Tavern Brawl" the clipping reveals:

> Several city police officers responding to a call to aid members of the Navy Shore Patrol in breaking up a tavern brawl near the U.S. Navy docks here last night got something of a surprise when they arrived on the scene to find the place empty of customers. According to a pair of very nervous waitresses, the Shore Patrol had arrived first and cleared the place out—but not before two of the sailors involved allegedly did a disappearing act. "They just sort of vanished into thin air...right there," reported one of the frightened hostesses, "and I ain't been drinking either!" At that point, according to her account, the Shore Patrol proceeded to hustle everybody out of the place in short order.[2]

Although the origin of the clipping may remain elusive, the same cannot be said for every aspect of the story concerning the so-called barroom brawl. It was during 1949 that a sailor named George Mayerchak was confined to the Philadelphia Navy Hospital for a month with a particularly bad bout of pneumonia. While he was there, Mayerchak began to hear stories from enlisted sailors concerning a strange event that had occurred at a local tavern near the Philadelphia Naval Yard in late 1943—an event that very closely fitted the contents of the newspaper clipping described by Moore and Berlitz. When Mayerchak went public with his story, he disputed the claim that the sailors in question disappeared without a trace, however; rather, he maintained, it was his understanding that instead they had briefly, and fantastically, flickered on and off. For our purposes here, the most important aspect of Mayerchak's recollections is that he heard these accounts no later than 1949—a full seven years before Carlos Allende told his amazing story to Morris Jessup.

Bill Moore also cited the testimony of one Harry Euton, who was reportedly involved in a Top Secret Second World War experiment to test a new concept of camouflaging ships against enemy radar. Euton told Moore that during the experiment something went catastrophically wrong and the ship literally became invisible to the naked eye from the second anti-aircraft mount to the rear of the vessel. As a result, it had no discernible bottom and no stern. Euton described to Moore the very strange and disorientating feeling of standing on the ship, but being unable to see it beneath his feet. He added that it was his automatic (and highly understandable) reaction to quickly reach out and grab something to keep him from falling: he clearly remembered holding tight to a cable or pipe, which felt normal, but which he could not see. Euton also told Moore that several crewmembers vanished in the blink of an eye, while others were still visible, but did not appear as they did normally—a potentially significant point upon which Euton steadfastly refused to clarify or even discuss any further.

Did the U.S. Navy really stumble upon the secrets of both invisibility and teleportation at the Philadelphia Naval Yard in 1943?

The Project Continues

The next chapter in the strange saga goes like this: Following the disastrous events that occurred in the Philadelphia Naval Yard in late 1943, the U.S. government moved quickly to shut down any and all research into such largely uncharted areas as invisibility and teleportation, primarily as a result of not having a full understanding and appreciation of the science behind what it was the Navy had stumbled upon. Deep, overriding fear of the unknown, in other words, was the prime motivation for halting this research. For a while, at least.

By 1952, rumors suggest, the times were changing; slowly at first, but ultimately at a rapid and mind-boggling pace. In that year, supposedly, some of the surviving military personnel and scientists who had been involved in the Philadelphia Experiment secretly got back together to discuss the possibility of once again trying to force open the doors to those strange realms of invisibility and teleportation—as well as seeking to understand what it was that had so drastically affected the mental and physical well-being of so many of the crewmembers of the USS *Eldridge*. They wanted to see if whatever had caused such terrible psychological effects could be used as a weapon to manipulate and/or disable the human brain. Mind control, in simplistic terms.

The U.S. Congress, however, members of which had been briefed on the less-than-positive outcome of the Philadelphia Experiment, nixed the entire program. Congress had major reservations about allowing Department of Defense scientists to recklessly dabble in fringe science that might very well end in unmitigated disaster for not only the research team, but for all of civilization as well. Thus, funding was duly, and swiftly, denied.

However, the Pentagon was not about to be thwarted by a bunch of old guys in suits who were closed-minded, stuck in their ways, and fearful of going where very few had gone before. Thus, a plot was initiated for the project to continue in stealth, far away from congressional oversight. Funding would have to come via alternative means. Much of the money for this project came from a huge stockpile of gold that had been liberated from the Nazis at the end of the Second World War, after having been found on a railroad car in France, close to the border with Switzerland. Utilizing such precious gold to fund military programs is certainly nothing new; it most definitely worked for Adolf Hitler during the Second World War, and it reportedly worked for the Montauk program too, a decade later.

So, with the money in place, and the scientists eager to push ahead, the project was ready to be taken to the next level. Allegedly, it first did so at the Brookhaven National Laboratory on Long Island, which came into existence in 1947, under the auspices of the Atomic Energy Commission, and whose work throughout the years has focused on high-energy physics. One of the vital requirements for the secondary project dealing with mind control was a large and powerful radar dish working on a specific frequency that could alter and manipulate human behavior. It so transpires that one was available on Long Island itself: at Montauk. The project was now beginning to take significant shape. According to the tales, it did way, way more than that.

Today, the legend of the Montauk Project has risen to astronomical levels. Since it began operating out of Montauk, we are assured, the team has come to understand to a significant degree the nature of time travel and time paradoxes, the secrets of teleportation, and the means by which both may be harnessed and utilized for secret military applications. Far stranger—indeed infinitely bizarre—stories indicate that decades after the Philadelphia Experiment of 1943 occurred, some of the Naval personnel who reportedly vanished into thin air at the time reappeared in the future, as a direct result of some form of fantastic time loop established between the 1943 project and its latter-day equivalent at Montauk.

Sounds like science fiction? Well, yes, it does. In fact, in 1984, a science-fiction movie titled, not surprisingly, *The Philadelphia Experiment*, was released, which took this scenario as its central theme. In the movie, two of the sailors involved in the 1943 test find themselves plunged into the heart of the mid-1980s, as a result of a time portal being opened between the Philadelphia Naval Yard of the past and a nearly identical secret, modern-era experiment. But there's much worse to come: the portal cannot be closed, and so the race is on to shut it down before the past and present fuse, resulting in Armageddon. Supporters of the Montauk story suggest that the movie was based upon a very real truth. Detractors suggest precisely the opposite, that the Montauk mythos was borne out of the movie.

Mind-Monsters

Scientists at Montauk involved in exploring the mysterious realms of the human mind supposedly uncovered something truly incredible: the ability to pull imagery from the depths of the human subconscious, externalize that imagery, and then allow it some form of quasi-existence in reality. In simple terms, nightmarish entities of the mind now had the ability to come to some degree of physical life. One longstanding story suggests a Bigfoot-type beast was manifested at Montauk by a man named Duncan Cameron, who reportedly possessed incredible mental skills and was a key player in the experimentation. Unfortunately, the beast slipped out of the control of its creator and ran riot at Montauk, before finally being reabsorbed or outright obliterated from existence.

With mind-monsters running wild and time portals threatening to destroy the world, science was out of control, and the team finally got cold feet. The entire project was abandoned as being too risky, and Montauk closed its doors to the past, the present, and maybe even to the future (if rumors of daring research into future-travel are true).

From Camp Hero to Montauk Air Force Station

Could there be any truth to these incredible tales? Or are they merely the ravings and rants of mentally deranged souls, shysters, and hucksters?

That a military base did exist at Montauk is not an issue of any doubt. As far back as the late 1700s, the eastern tip of Long Island was considered a point of strategic military importance. Initially, and throughout the period of the War of Independence, it acted as a prime lookout point for hostile British forces. Then, during the First World War, the same locale played host to military personnel and spy balloons, all keeping a careful watch for hordes of invading Germans. In early 1942, in direct response to the tragedy of Pearl Harbor in December 1941, as well as the fact that Nazi submarines were perceived as significant threats to East Coast cities, factories, and military installations, the U.S. government finally gave the go-ahead for the construction of an impressively sized official facility, replete with bunkers, at Montauk. It became known as Camp Hero.

To ensure that it did not attract too much unwanted attention—particularly from Nazi spies that might very well have been hovering around—the entire installation was ingeniously disguised as a pleasant little fishing port. A secret military outpost was the *last* thing anyone had on their mind when viewing Camp Hero from the sea. After the end of the war in 1945 the base became largely obsolete. That is, until it became apparent that the Soviets were seemingly intent on dominating the planet. Soon new plans were formulated for Camp Hero, including a name change in 1948 to Montauk Point, and, five years later, to the Montauk Air Force Station.

By the mid-to-late 1950s, Montauk was an integral part of efforts to watch for, and thwart, a Soviet sneak attack on the United States. Despite various changes in names, functional capabilities, and activities, it continued to play this role during the Cold War, particularly as a result of its radar-based capabilities. In 1978, President

Jimmy Carter ordered the base closed, chiefly due to the fact that satellite-based technology was rapidly taking the place of radar. The death knell for Montauk officially came on the very last day of January 1981. (Unless you subscribe to the notion that certain work, into such areas as time travel, invisibility, and teleportation, continued in secret.)

The Degaussing Story

With Montauk's background now laid out, let's address the base's reputed role as one of the United States's most secret locations, perhaps even surpassing Area 51 in terms of strange goings-on. To do that we need to go back to the beginning: the Philadelphia Experiment.

As was noted earlier in this chapter, when the tales of Carlos Allende first surfaced, the U.S. Navy maintained they were nothing more than outrageous fantasy, with absolutely zero basis in reality. Today, more than half a century after Allende popped into public view, the Navy tells a significantly different story. Although there is certainly no official endorsement of the stories that the USS *Eldridge* was rendered invisible and teleported from one locale to another and then back again, or that crewmembers were injured, killed, or outright vanished into oblivion in October 1943, the Navy does admit that, in all likelihood, the story has a basis in a secret of real significance.

The Navy's current position reads as follows: "Personnel at the Fourth Naval District believe that the questions surrounding the so-called Philadelphia Experiment arise from quite routine research which occurred during World War II at the Philadelphia Naval

Shipyard. Until recently, it was believed that the foundation for the apocryphal stories arose from degaussing experiments which have the effect of making a ship undetectable or 'invisible' to magnetic mines."[3]

Degaussing, in simple terms, is a process in which a system of electrical cables is installed around the circumference of a ship's hull, running from bow to stern on both sides. An electrical current is then passed through these cables to cancel out the ship's magnetic field.

"Degaussing equipment," says the Navy, "was installed in the hull of ships and could be turned on whenever the ship was in waters that might contain magnetic mines, usually shallow waters in combat areas. It could be said that degaussing, correctly done, makes a ship 'invisible' to the sensors of magnetic mines, but the ship remains visible to the human eye, radar, and underwater listening devices."[4]

Just to confuse things, the Navy has offered a *further* theory to explain what might lie at the heart of the story: "Another likely genesis of the bizarre stories about levitation, teleportation and effects on human crewmembers might be attributed to experiments with the generating plant of a destroyer, the USS *Timmerman*. In the 1950s, this ship was part of an experiment to test the effects of a small, high frequency generator providing 1000hz, instead of the standard 400hz. The higher frequency generator produced corona discharges, and other well-known phenomena associated with high frequency generators. None of the crew suffered effects from the experiment."[5]

The fact that the Navy first denounced the Philadelphia Experiment as having *no* basis in reality, and today is seemingly happy to offer no less than *two* theories to explain what might have been behind the legend—both involving verifiable secret projects—has inevitably raised suspicions that we are still not being told the full truth of what really occurred all those years ago at that mysterious naval yard. Could that truth really have had something to do with classified research into invisibility?

Provable classified research

It is a verifiable reality that in the 1940s the U.S. Navy was secretly working on a project codenamed Yahootie, the goal of which was to develop an invisible aircraft. By early 1942, it had become clear to the Navy that its aerial bombers were far too slow to visually spot a German U-boat submarine cruising on the surface and successfully launch an attack during daylight hours; U-boat commanders would frequently spot the lumbering bombers and dive beneath the ocean in plenty of time to avoid destruction. As a result, military planners came up with an ingenious idea: they placed a row of bright lights on the wings and propeller hubs of several experimental aircraft, which could be adjusted by their crews to match the natural background light of the sky. This, then, was essentially a means of camouflage rather than literal invisibility.

Investigative writer Charles R. Smith noted in 2005 that "The U.S. may very well possess an advanced version of Yahootie." Smith continued that the aircraft in question "reportedly uses a combination of lights, low-noise engines and radar-absorbing skin to render itself practically invisible in daylight...."[6] Similarly, the British Ministry of Defense has admitted that it has been secretly funding a project known as Chameleon that is designed to diminish the contrast between an aircraft and the sky.

What of the reportedly Top Secret research undertaken at the Philadelphia Naval Yard in 1943, and years later at Montauk, into the realm of teleportation? Is there any hard evidence to suggest elements of the U.S. government really have researched this particular phenomenon, which many are content to relegate to the world of on-screen science fiction?

In August 2004, the U.S. Air Force declassified into the public domain a document titled "The Teleportation Physics Study." The report was the work of a man named Eric W. Davis, of a Las Vegas–based outfit called Warp Drive Metrics, which the Air Force Research Laboratory (AFRL), Air Force Materiel Command had quietly contracted to explore the strange realm of teleportation. Within the pages of the report (which became Air Force property when the work was completed) Davis noted, "This study was tasked with the purpose of collecting information describing the teleportation of material objects, providing a description of teleportation as it occurs in physics, its theoretical and experimental status, and a projection of potential applications."[7]

The Davis report noted that there did indeed appear to be keen interest, in official circles, in teleportation and its potential applications by the Department of Defense: "...it became known to Dr. [Robert Lull] Forward [a now-deceased physicist] and myself, along with several colleagues both inside and outside of government, that anomalous teleportation has been scientifically investigated and separately documented by the Department of Defense."[8]

When the Air Force declassified the study, Lawrence Krauss of Case Western Reserve University, the author of *The Physics of Star Trek*, stated: "It is in large part crackpot physics," and added that it contained "some things adapted from reasonable theoretical studies, and other things from nonsensical ones."[9]

Perhaps the Air Force, after reading Davis's document, agreed: "The views expressed in the report are those of the author and do not necessarily reflect the official policy of the Air Force, the Department of Defense or the U.S. Government," was the statement made by the Air Force's Research Laboratory when questioned by *USA Today*. Asked why the laboratory had secretly sponsored the study, AFRL spokesman Ranney Adams said, "If we don't turn over stones, we don't know if we have missed something." Significantly, the AFRL added, "There are no plans by the AFRL Propulsion Directorate for additional funding on this contract."[10] Not surprisingly, this latter statement was perceived by some Montauk researchers as evidence that the military was trying to publicly distance itself from teleportation research, while privately continuing to dig deeper into it.

Holographic Imagery

As for Bigfoot, and the notion that the Montauk team learned how to project imagery of such beasts from the dark depths of the human mind into quasi-physical form in the real world, isn't that just too outlandish to warrant even a solitary comment? Not everyone thinks so. One of those who offered commentary on these matters is a man who features significantly in another chapter of this book: Gabe Valdez, a key player in the story of the alleged underground alien base at Dulce, New Mexico.

Valdez has uncovered information that leads him to believe that many New Mexico Bigfoot sightings are actually the work of a covert arm of the U.S. government possessing the ability to create holographic imagery of the hairy man-beasts. The purpose? To deter people from getting too close to some of its secret underground installations. It is fascinating to hear such a theory coming out of the mouth of a respected police officer who was consulted by the FBI on cattle-mutilation cases at Dulce in the 1970s. Even more fascinating, Valdez's position on Bigfoot eerily parallels the stories surfacing from the Montauk research community.

TIME Travel

There is one other major area of controversy in relation to Montauk we've yet to cover: time travel. Although the idea that government agencies may be utilizing secret bases to research the possibility of surfing the centuries back and forth sounds, to most people, like nothing more than an adventure-packed movie, some have suggested that fact is far stranger than anything that could ever be conjured up by even the most imaginative Hollywood scriptwriters.

Dr. David Lewis Anderson—of the New Mexico–based Anderson Institute, a division of Anderson Multinational LLC, whose primary goal is "the development of time-warped field theory, its application, and ensuring the ongoing development of time reactor system design concepts and capabilities"[11]—has stated that, decades ago, he spent time working on a secret project at the U.S. Air Force's Flight Test Center at Edwards Air Force Base in California. The goal of the project was definitive time travel. We may never know the extent to which success has been achieved in this particularly strange area, but we do have this on-the-record source revealing that it has at least been investigated.

closed for business?

Today, the Montauk installation is no longer in use. In 2002 it was renamed the Camp Hero State Park, and is now widely open to the general public. Its role in classified activity is over—unless, that is, as many Montauk enthusiasts fully accept, far below the old base, dark and strange experimentation still continues at a steady pace, far away from both prying eyes and congressional oversight.

Given that we now know that official agencies of the U.S. government and the military *have* undertaken research into invisibility, time travel, teleportation, and even the mystery of Bigfoot, perhaps we might be wise to muse upon an interesting scenario: the Montauk program was not all fiction. Just maybe, Montauk is not as dead as the powers that be would have us believe. Perhaps, in some secret domain underneath Long Island, the sensational truth still exists, guarded with extreme prejudice by those tasked with ensuring the public never learns the incredible truths behind the mysteries of Montauk.

c - 15

WEATHERING THE STORM

c - 15

MIDWAY THROUGH 1996, THE UNITED STATES Air Force announced the publication of what was termed the USAF 2025 report. Prepared by the 2025 Support Office at the Air University, Air Education and Training Command, and developed by the Air University Press, Educational Services Directorate, College of Aerospace Doctrine, Research, and Education, at Maxwell Air Force Base, Alabama, the report was, to quote the military, "a study designed to comply with a directive from the chief of staff of the Air Force to examine the concepts, capabilities, and technologies the United States will require to remain the dominant air and space force in the future."[1]

Warfare and the weather: A hurricane, as seen from space.

One particularly intriguing subsection of the report had the notable title of "Weather as a Force Multiplier: Owning the Weather in 2025." That's correct: the U.S. military has been hard at work trying to determine if the manipulation and even creation of harsh weather conditions—such as hurricanes, earthquakes, volcanoes, and other forms of devastation that are normally ascribed to nature—might be considered a viable tool of warfare in the very near future.

In the astounding words of the Air Force's most learned forward-thinkers of the mid-1990s: "In 2025, U.S. aerospace forces can 'own the weather' by capitalizing on emerging technologies and focusing development of those technologies to war-fighting applications. While some segments of society will always be reluctant to examine controversial issues such as weather-modification, the tremendous military capabilities that could result from this field are ignored at our own peril. Weather-modification offers the war fighter a wide-range of possible options to defeat or coerce an adversary."[2]

The Air Force also noted, "The desirability to modify storms to support military objectives is the most aggressive and controversial type of weather-modification. While offensive weather-modification efforts would certainly be undertaken by U.S. forces with great caution and trepidation, it is clear that we cannot afford to allow an adversary to obtain an exclusive weather-modification capability."[3]

The Air Force was not the only area of officialdom expressing interest in and concerns about weather-modification technologies for specific use in warfare. On April 28, 1997, the U.S. Secretary of Defense William S. Cohen delivered the keynote speech at the University of Georgia–based Conference on Terrorism, Weapons of Mass Destruction, and U.S. Strategy, and intriguingly warned the audience that there were powerful, shadowy forces out there who were "engaging in an eco-type of terrorism whereby they can alter the climate, set off earthquakes, volcanoes remotely through the use of Electro-Magnetic waves. So there are plenty of ingenious minds out there that are at work finding ways in which they can wreak terror upon other nations. It's real."[4]

HAARP

The big questions are: to what extent have such technologies gone beyond the theoretical and been successfully (clandestinely) developed? Is such technology already being secretly utilized on a planet-wide scale, in order to instill fear in, and exert control over, the world's population, and also exert military control and influence over areas of strategic interest? Many conspiracy theorists say yes. The target of their accusations is a sensitive, Department of Defense installation in Alaska that is home to a project shrouded in deep controversy: HAARP, or the High Frequency Active Auroral Research Program. In the words of scientists at the U.S. Air Force Research Laboratory, who coordinate the work of HAARP along with the U.S. Navy's Office of Naval Research and Naval Research Laboratory as well as the Defense Advanced Research Projects Agency (DARPA), the project is designed to "analyze the ionosphere and investigate the potential for developing ionospheric enhancement technology for radio communications and surveillance purposes."[5]

Based at the HAARP Research Station near Gakona, the project is seen by many as an even more terrifying Alaskan phenomenon than Sarah Palin, which surely serves to indicate the profound levels of anxiety that surround the project within those realms where the conspiracy-minded lurk. As well as its legitimate involvement in analyzing the ionosphere and studying its potential for developing ionospheric enhancement technology for radio communications and surveillance purposes, HAARP staff perform other tasks, too, such as analyzing weather-related issues and "long-term variations in the ozone layer."[6] The fact that most of this work is undertaken by military agencies is one of the reasons why so many suspicions surround HAARP.

It could be argued that HAARP's overwhelming military link is not so strange; after all, in today's world, with an ever-increasing reliance upon ever-advancing technologies, fluctuations in the ionosphere—which commences roughly 35 miles above the surface of our planet—might adversely affect military communications systems, particularly so in emergency situations.

Those behind HAARP are keenly aware of the conspiracy theories that surround the program, and have specifically, and carefully, made their position clear on why there is so much involvement on the part of the U.S. Department of Defense in its operations: "Interest in ionosphere research at HAARP stems both from the large number of communication, surveillance and navigation systems that have radio paths which pass through the ionosphere, and from the unexplored potential of technological innovations which suggest applications such as detecting underground objects, communicating to great depths in the sea or earth, and generating infrared and optical emissions."[7]

Those who see HAARP as having a distinctly covert agenda, however, point to what they consider the projects' darkest of all secrets.

The Earthquake in Haiti

On Tuesday, January 12, 2010, the Caribbean country of Haiti was hit by a devastating earthquake that killed more than 300,000 people, injured approximately the same amount, and left more than a million people homeless. It was a terrible, shocking tragedy for the people of Haiti, and one from which, even at the time I write these words, the nation is still struggling to fully recover. And, in the wake of the carnage, it did not take long at all for conspiracy theorists to suggest that the reckless—some even suggested the cold and deliberate—actions of HAARP personnel were to blame.

Just 48 hours after the Haitian events occurred, the Website Ahrcanum (*www.ahrcanum.wordpress.com*), which covers such issues as New World Order fears, weather-modification technologies, and conspiracy theories relative to the swine flu controversy, among many other topics, devoted much Web space to a discussion of the events at issue, and whether or not HAARP staff, using technologies that might have the ability to induce and target earthquakes in specific areas of the planet, were the actual culprits. Although such a theory might provoke the rolling of eyes in the majority of people, it should not be forgotten that, back in 1997, none other than U.S. Defense Secretary Cohen had specifically warned about hostile forces that might soon possess the technology to deliberately stimulate earthquakes.

The Ahrcanum article provoked a wealth of online debate and response. Some pointed to the fact that immediately after the disaster occurred, U.S. military personnel descended on Haiti en-masse to deliver assistance, food, clothing, and medical supplies, as a means to help the populace recover from the disaster—not everyone was so sure that the reason behind this effort was as altruistic as most people assumed. Commentators at the Ahrcanum site came right out and suggested that the earthquake was a deliberate HAARP-induced event, designed to provide the United States government with a reason to make its presence strongly felt in an area in which it had special interests. One concerned writer asserted at the Website, "Haiti is going to be the next U.S. colony."

But why would anyone want to colonize, or even exert control over Haiti? What would be the reason? After all, it's hardly a nation equipped with nuclear-tipped missiles aimed at the United States. Its people are not planning dirty-bomb attacks on U.S. soil. And Haiti is most certainly not in a position to launch a large-scale military assault on America, even if it wanted to. However, Haiti does have something that many nations lack: substantial oil reserves. Currently, the island is estimated to be home to 3 million barrels of off-shore oil. More significantly, the Greater Antilles, which includes Cuba, Haiti, Puerto Rico, and the Dominican Republic, have a combined estimated 142 million barrels of oil, and 159 billion cubic feet of gas, according to a U.S. Geological Survey report in 2000. The authors of the USGS report speculated that the levels might actually be much, much greater: perhaps more than 900 million barrels of oil, and more than a *trillion* cubic feet of gas.

And guess what: HAARP technology can remotely sense the mineral content of the planet's subsurface. In other words, in plain, easy-to-understand English, HAARP can be secretly utilized to find underground and undersea oil reserves. Conspiracy theorists say that both Afghanistan and Iraq have large reserves of oil, but the hostilities in the Middle East have already allowed U.S. military forces to occupy both countries, and, as a result, hold some sway over the oil supply of both. But what about countries deeply rich in oil that are *not* showing hostility to the United States? How might they be successfully occupied and their oil supplies targeted and perhaps even manipulated in the future? The theorists say that when large deposits of oil have been found by

HAARP, and there is no military justification for invading the relevant country, HAARP's earthquake-inducing technology has been used to provoke a seeming natural disaster that has then allowed officialdom to move in with what looks like a friendly offer of help.

To be sure, this is a highly controversial and massively damning scenario, but—as far as the HAARP-watchers are concerned—it's seen as a wholly viable one. And in a world where oil reserves are becoming ever more depleted, such a technology is not just important; it may prove vital in determining which nations survive and which go under in the undoubtedly fraught decades and centuries ahead of us. Make no mistake: our current, overwhelming reliance upon oil *will* pose major challenges in the years to come.

As a perfect example of the situation in which even now we find ourselves, in 2007, a U.S. diplomat met with one Sadad al-Husseini, a geologist and the former head of the Saudi oil monopoly, Aramco. Husseini said, in bleak terms, that Saudi oil output would likely reach its peak production point in the next few years, after which the rate of production would decline *very* noticeably. Precisely how fast that downward journey might be is, right now, open to much debate. We might, however, be able to glean more than a few ideas from a report titled "Peaking of World Oil Production: Impacts, Mitigation, and Risk Management" that was prepared by Robert Hirsch for the U.S. Department of Energy and published in February 2005.

Consider the following extract from the report: "The peaking of world oil production presents the U.S. and the world with an unprecedented risk management problem.

As peaking is approached, liquid fuel prices and price volatility will increase dramatically, and, without timely mitigation, the economic, social, and political costs will be unprecedented."[8]

That one stark word alone—*unprecedented*—should give us at least some idea of how our world might radically change once oil goes belly-up.

The Tsunami in Japan

In the wake of the even more tragic events that devastated Japan on March 11, 2011—involving a pulverizing earthquake, a tsunami that provoked ocean waves of more than 120 feet, and a meltdown at the Fukushima 1 and Fukushima 2 Nuclear Power Plants that led to more than 12,000 deaths and a nation stunned into shock and disbelief—online conspiracy theorists expressed concern when 20,000 U.S. military personnel, 19 Naval craft, and 120 aircraft, via an operation called Tomodachi (*friend*, in Japanese), took a leading role in handling the crisis.

Once again, a theory was suggested that the friendly, humanitarian assistance was in reality a cover to allow U.S. forces to increase their presence in an area of the globe deemed to be of strategic and military value. And, said the same conspiracy theorists, what better way to subtly—and seemingly innocently—ensure one's influence in an area of keen interest than via a selfless mission of mercy? If the conspiracy crowd were correct in their views on HAARP, could oil have been a motivating factor here, too?

As of 2010, Japan had state-controlled oil reserves in excess of 300 million barrels, and privately owned reserves that exceeded 120 million barrels. Interestingly, however, way back on February 21, 1922, the *New York Times* published an article titled "Experts Say Japan has 300 Years' Oil," with a subtitle of "Engineers Estimate that American Reserves will be Exhausted in 20 Years." The newspaper quoted from a new report prepared for the American Institute of Mining and Metallurgical Engineers that, in part, said, "Considering her actual requirements, it appears that Japan is more fortunate than most nations in the possession of oil reserves in the future. Japan possesses much more oil than her propagandists have tried to make the world believe she has."[9]

Of course, U.S. oil was not depleted by 1944, as the article alarmingly suggested it might be. And back in 1922 it would have been pretty much impossible to predict how Japan's reliance on oil would increase, to the point where that 300-years scenario became utterly useless. Nevertheless, the idea that Japan may secretly possess far more oil than many have even begun to realize is, if nothing else, significant food for thought.

The worrying reality is that of the 21 largest oil fields on the planet, no less than nine are already in steady, irreversible decline. Finding new reserves of oil, and controlling access to those same reserves, may prove vital in determining the fate of whole countries as the decades progress. And just maybe, say some at least, HAARP is playing a fundamental role in a secret race for future survival; a future that, if not somehow averted, might see the lights forever extinguished, our oil-reliant vehicles utterly extinct, and civilization in chaos and savagery.

E.M. Fields

HAARP has also become the target of people who see its actions as being wholly nefarious in nature for another, very different reason, but no less disturbing in scope. Aside from the HAARP staff themselves, there is probably no one who knows more about the project—and the dark theories regarding what many accept that its personnel may really be doing—than Dr. Nick Begich, Jr., the son of Democratic Party member of the U.S. House of Representatives from Alaska, Nicholas Joseph Begich, Sr., who was presumed killed when the Cessna 310 plane he was flying in on October 16, 1972 vanished without trace during a flight from Anchorage to Juneau. Begich Jr.'s brother is Mark Begich, currently the junior U.S. Senator for the state of Alaska. As for Nick Begich, as well as having been twice elected President of the Alaska Federation of Teachers and the Anchorage Council of Education, he is the co-author, with Jeanne Manning, of the illuminating book *Angels Don't Play This Haarp*, which is a deeply unsettling exposé of the HAARP program.

Begich said that whereas HAARP personnel are keen to impress upon people that the program is chiefly an academic project with the intent to alter the ionosphere to upgrade communications for our own benefit, there is another side to the story. He noted that as far back as 1996, the U.S. government had assigned no less than $15 million to HAARP to develop Earth- penetrating tomography, or imaging of the planet's subsurface. The problem with all this, Begich said, is that "[the particular frequency required for] Earth-penetrating radiations is within the frequency range most cited for disruption of human mental functions. It may also have profound effects on migration patterns of fish and wild animals which rely on an undisturbed energy field to find their routes."[10]

The U.S. Air Force—a central player in the HAARP program—has long been aware of these effects that Begich has warned about for years. One of many official USAF documents on such matters spells out the disturbing facts: "The potential applications of artificial electromagnetic fields are wide-ranging. Some of these potential uses include dealing with terrorist groups, crowd control, controlling breaches of security at military installations, and antipersonnel techniques in tactical warfare. In all of these cases the EM (electromagnetic) systems would be used to produce mild to severe physiological disruption or perceptual distortion or disorientation. In addition, the ability of individuals to function could be degraded to such a point that they would be combat-ineffective."[11]

That the work of HAARP may have significant, adverse side-effects on the human nervous system and psychological state is highly worrying. But there is another issue too. Begich's discoveries that HAARP's work could conceivably have adverse effects on the migratory routes of certain animals has led a number of commentators to suggest that the unsettling, planet-wide wave of bird and fish deaths that were heavily reported on by the world's media in the latter part of 2010 and early 2011 were the result of wild and reckless HAARP operations.

It was during this clearly delineated period that literally hundreds of red-winged blackbirds were found dead in Louisiana, countless blackbirds met their deaths under unusual circumstances in Arkansas, and tens of thousands of fish turned up lifeless in the Arkansas River. On top of that, more than 50 Jackdaws were found dead, lying on the ground in Sweden; at least 200 birds of varying types were discovered on a Texas bridge; and no less than 40,000 devil crabs died under mysterious circumstances off the coast of England.

Some scientists and elements of officialdom struggled to place all the mystifying deaths into wholly down-to-earth categories—such as the rigors of nature, the extremes of weather, and man-made pollution—but others suggested this collectively pointed towards a looming apocalypse of Old Testament proportions. Some quietly—and more than a few not so quietly—suggested that HAARP was to blame. On this latter point, on January 5, 2011, Steve Cooper of the Conservative Monster Website published an article titled "Was HAARP Missile Defense Test Behind Massive Bird Deaths?" It was this paper that provoked a flurry of online debate about what HAARP was up to, and how our world faced potential collapse and destruction as a result of the crazed actions of an elite group of harebrained scientists up north.

$\bigcirc$

The debate concerning the strange, massive die-offs of animals from late 2010 to early 2011, the theoretical links between HAARP and earthquake activity around the globe, and HAARP's alleged tie-in with the scrambling of the U.S. government to secure what may be left of the oil-reserves continues to rage online, at conferences, within the pages of magazines, and on radio-talk-shows where the conspiracy-obsessed like to hang out. Whether HAARP really *is* up to something truly abhorrent—and on a worldwide scale, no less—or if an earthquake is sometimes just an earthquake, and the numerous deaths of animals are merely the tragic results of the harshness of nature, depends to a great degree on whose conclusions you accept as being the valid or most likely ones. Until we do have a firm answer, it seems certain that conspiracy researchers will continue to harp on about what's really afoot in the Alaskan wilderness.

CONCLUSIONS

OUR LONG AND WINDING JOURNEY INTO THE strange and enigmatic world of myriad underground bases, nearly impenetrable installations, undersea realms, and even alleged lunar outposts is now at its close. What can we say about the multitude of worldwide secret sites that have come under our close scrutiny? Clearly, there is a degree of division between what we know as undeniable fact, what we think we know, and what many still might consider the stuff of rumor, theory, hearsay, and unproved, outrageous conspiracy-mongering.

That well-guarded installations such as Fort Detrick, Maryland; Porton Down, England; and Utah's Dugway Proving Ground do exist is not in any doubt whatsoever.

And that they have, for decades, been steeped in matters of profound controversy is also a matter of official record. Biological warfare programs, research into exotic viruses, and suspicious deaths—of people and animals—are all demonstrable and provable.

When it comes to other super-secret sites, trying to unravel fact from fiction, and government-orchestrated disinformation from exaggeration, is somewhat more problematic. Take Nevada's Area 51, for example: The base is clearly there, and there is probably barely a soul on the planet who has not heard of it. But is it really home to captured alien spacecraft, as the stories Bob Lazar suggest? Or is the UFO angle merely an ingenious ruse promoted and encouraged by officialdom to hide its far more down-to-earth research into novel aircraft designs? The jury, if we are truly honest with ourselves, must still be out.

It's very much the same with Hangar 18: Enough credible sources—such as U.S. Senator Barry Goldwater and CIA high-ranker Victor Marchetti—have spoken out on the UFO secrets of Wright-Patterson AFB to demonstrate that *something* weird is afoot at the base, and has been for a very long time. Hell, the quest for the truth about Wright-Pat's little men nearly put computer-hacker Matthew Bevan behind bars for a significant number of years. But are those little men and their attendant ships from the stars the real thing, or are they only tales designed to keep the UFO faithful far away from advanced military technologies of a specifically human kind? Questions abound. Hard answers, typically, do not.

Then there are the disturbing tales of Dulce, New Mexico, of the secret realms below London's Underground rail system, and of the undersea, alien kingdom said to exist off the coast of Puerto Rico. These stories collectively suggest that some secret, below-surface installations, known to the respective governments under whose land they exist, specifically operate outside of the control of our leaders. In short, stark terms: our presidents, our prime ministers, and our royal families have catastrophically lost control of what is afoot in the deep, winding tunnels of London, in the vast caves and caverns of New Mexico, and in and around the deep waters of the Caribbean. Maybe that's the reason for the total secrecy about some such secret places: not that officialdom is clandestinely running the show, but that officialdom has been unceremoniously kicked out, forcibly removed, or outright denied access by the nonhuman entities that have considered the dark abodes to be their personal property from pretty much day one.

As for the idea that a secret base could exist on the moon: well, at first glance it admittedly stretches credibility to the limit—maybe even *beyond* the limit! At second glance, however, things are somewhat different. We now know that 50 years ago the U.S. Army was quietly looking to construct just such a facility on the lunar surface, via its ambitious Project Horizon plan. Karl Wolfe has disclosed truly astounding data relative to a huge alien installation on the far side of the Moon. And remote-viewer Ingo Swann, whose links to the secret world of government involvement in ESP espionage operations is a matter of official record, has told a fascinating, cloak-and-dagger story about official knowledge of a vast moon-based facility belonging to...well, *someone*. What we have here is a high degree of smoke. The attendant fire, if we are determined to find it, may possibly be within our very grasp. The vast majority of us do not possess the ability to literally travel to the moon to locate the base and confirm its existence, but securing the testimony of further Karl Wolfes, and more Ingo Swanns may, in the long haul, be the next best thing.

Moving on to the 2012 controversy, there's no doubt that there has been an undeniable increase in the construction of secure installations in the wake of the events of September 11, 2001. And there is also no doubt that much of this construction is designed to offer protection to the elite of the government, the military, and the intelligence community, in the event of a catastrophic emergency. Whether that emergency is a known one that officialdom has been able to pinpoint and to verify, such as whatever the Mayas predicted would happen in 2012, or if the planning is due to a wholly theoretical future event of disastrous proportions—possibly one instigated by terrorists involving the much-feared dirty-bombs—is unclear. But given that 2012 is looming perilously close, matters should become clear very soon.

In all likelihood, the construction of secret sites, classified installations, and covert government and military facilities will continue at an ever-increasing pace. Xe Services LLC, formerly known as Blackwater USA and Blackwater Worldwide, operates essentially as a private military company that, presently, is the largest of the U.S. State Department's three private-security contractors, and had a remarkable track record (but for all the *wrong* reasons) in helping to maintain security in Iraq during the last decade. That hasn't stopped Xe Services LLC from forging ahead with its own sensitive installations, however. For example, their "United States Training Center," which takes up 7,000 acres of land in northeastern North Carolina, provides expert training for U.S. military and government personnel. It offers hand-to-hand-combat programs, as well as courses focused upon tactical driving—or, rather, how to get the hell out of a dicey situation when terrorist bullets are slamming into the trunk of your armored car. Given that Xe Services LLC is forging ahead on a massively ambitious scale, the probability is that we will see them operating to a far greater degree both within and without the United States.

It looks as though the general public is trying to get in on the secret base action too. Given the decidedly shaky world stage that exists right now—one that is seemingly overwhelmed by earthquakes, tsunamis, wars, and the specter of 2012—people pretty much all over the globe want to have their own fortified places in which to hide out if the countdown to the end really does begin. Right now, Hardened Structures, a company that operates out of Virginia Beach, is doing a veritable killing in terms of sales of its fortified locales and underground bunkers. Californians are ordering fallout shelters from the company to cope with what they see as a radioactive disaster hitting the United States as a result of the nuclear meltdowns in Japan during early 2011. Others are worried that a coming economic collapse in the United States will provoke a need for the average family to have its very own secret, underground structure in which to hide out when the country teeters, collapses, and ultimately flatlines beyond recovery. Notably, Hardened Structures' CEO, Brian Camden, acknowledged in March 2011 that many of the orders his company had received were primarily in relation to "2012, end-of-the-world-as-you-know-it kind of stuff." He was careful to note, however, that: "We don't subscribe to any kind of scenario...the only thing we know for sure, is that no one knows what's going to happen."[1]

Well, maybe *someone* knows, even if it's not Hardened Structures.

In April 2011, extensive digging began at the White House in the vicinity of the famous West Wing. Ostensibly, the media was informed, the work was strictly renovation-based, and focused upon repairing and upgrading sewer systems, water pipes, and electrical systems. Such proclamations, however, were viewed somewhat skeptically by certain elements of the Washington press corps. Although the East Wing of the White House sits atop a hardened bunker designed to survive a nuclear attack on the nation's capital—it's called the Presidential Emergency Operations Center (PEOC)—the idea that the new work on the West Wing was somehow linked to the PEOC, and that elaborate tunneling was being undertaken to expand, strengthen, and deepen the facility, was openly scoffed at by White House officials and spokespersons. Some who followed the story suggested the White House scoffed just a little bit *too* much.

Whatever the truth behind these very latest developments in the world of secret government bunkers, bases, and installations, I will say this in closing: As our world, our civilization, and our society heads off into Orwellian territory, the likelihood is that you're going to see a certain pair of words more and more, and just about everywhere you go. They are, of course: *Keep Out!*

NOTES

chapter 1

1. Friedman, "Bob Lazar."
2. "Element 115."
3. Haines, "Die-Hard."
4. Good, *Alien Liaison*.

chapter 2

1. Redfern, "UFOs on Radar."
2. Warren and Robbins, *Left at East Gate*.

3. Ibid.
4. Good, *Alien Liaison*.

chapter 3

1. Erickson, "U.S. Army."
2. Committee on Veterans' Affairs, *Is Military Research Hazardous*.
3. Bragalia, "Is this where."
4. Bauman, "Is Dugway's expansion."

chapter 4

1. Slany and Eizenstat, "U.S. and Allied."
2. Ibid.

chapter 5

1. Goldwater, Letter to Schlomo Arnon.
2. United States Air Force, "Unidentified."
3. Stringfield, *Situation Red*.
4. Stringfield, *UFO Crash/Retrievals*.

chapter 6

1. Redfern, Interview with Frank Wiley.
2. Ibid.
3. Ibid.
4. Lowe, *Tunnel Vision*.
5. Kilgallen, "Flying Saucer."

chapter 7

1. Department of Defense, "Conduct."
2. Ryan and Kerry, "A Letter."
3. U.S. Fish and Wildlife, "White-Nose."
4. Ibid.

chapter 8

1. Federal Bureau, "Animal."
2. Ibid.
3. Ibid.
4. Ibid.
5. Ibid.
6. Hamilton, *Cosmic*.

chapter 10

1. Steiger, *Monsters*.
2. Ibid.
3. Oaks, "Paranormal."
4. Redfern, Interview with Mac Tonnies.
5. Ibid.
6. Guest, "The Other."
7. Pope, *Operation*.
8. Ibid.

chapter 11

1. United States Army, "Project Horizon Report: Volume I."
2. Dolan, "Musings."

chapter 12

1. Roberts, *UFO Down?*
2. Dodd, *Alien Investigator*.
3. Redfern, *Cosmic Crashes*.
4. Ibid.
5. Redfern, Interview with Ministry of Defense source.
6. Meek, "FBI was told."
7. Jordan, "Senator."

chapter 13

1. Caribbean Primate Research Center.
2. Austin, "Manned Undersea Structures."

chapter 14

1. Genzlinger, *Jessup Dimension*.
2. Berlitz and Moore, *Philadelphia Experiment*.
3. United States Navy, "Information Sheet."
4. United States Navy, "Philadelphia Experiment."
5. United States Navy, "Information Sheet."
6. Smith, Charles, "UFO Secrets."
7. Davis, "Teleportation."

8. Ibid.

9. Vergano, "Air Force."

10. Ibid.

11. "About the Anderson Institute."

chapter 15

1. United States Air Force, "Air Force 2025."

2. Ibid.

3. Ibid.

4. U.S. Department of Defense, "DoD News."

5. High Frequency.

6. Ibid.

7. Ibid.

8. Hirsch, "Peaking."

9. "Experts Say."

10. "Are We in a HAARP."

11. Tyler, *Intensity Conflict*.

conclusions

1. Hickey, "Underground Bunkers."

BIBLIO GRAPHY

Note: All Websites were last reviewed in April 2011.

"A Future Armageddon? Yamantau Mountain Complex." *www.bibliotecapleyades.net/sociopolitica/esp_socio-pol_underground16.htm*.

"About the Anderson Institute." *www.andersoninstitute. com/about-the-anderson-institute.html*, 2011.

"An American Werewolf in London." IMDB.com. *www.imdb.com/title/tt0082010/*.

"Amerithrax or Anthrax Investigation." FBI.gov, 2011. *www.fbi.gov/about-us/history/famous-cases/anthrax-amerithrax/amerithrax-investigation*.

Andrews, Steve. "Sadad al Husseini sees peak in 2015." *Energy Bulletin*, September 14, 2005. *www.energybulletin.net/node/9498*.

"Animal Mutilation." The FBI: Federal Bureau of Investigation, March 2011. *vault.fbi.gov/Animal%20 Mutilation*.

"Are we in a HAARP Earthquake War?" *beforeitsnews.com/story/20/951/Are_We_in_a_HAARP_Earthquake_War.html*, May 5, 2010.

"Are Your Secrets Safe?" *Dateline NBC*, October 27, 1992.

"Area 51 of Russia." *www.militaryphotos.net/forums/archive/index.php/t-192784.html*, January 17, 2011.

Austin, C.F., and U.S. Naval Ordnance Test Station China Lake CA. "Manned Undersea Structures—The Rock-Site Concept." DTIC Online. *oai.dtic.mil/oai/oa i?verb=getRecord&metadataPrefix=html&identifier= AD0803366*, October 1966.

Baker, Alan. *Invisible Eagle*. London: Virgin Books, 2000.

Baker, Norman. "Why I know weapons expert Dr. David Kelly was murdered, by the MP who spent a year investigating his death." *Daily Mail*, October 20, 2007. *www.dailymail.co.uk/news/article-488667/ Why-I-know-weapons-expert-Dr-David-Kelly-murdered-MP-spent-year-investigating-death.html*.

Bauman, Joe. "Is Dugway's expansion an alien concept?" *Deseret News*, November 4, 2004. *www.deseretnews.com/article/595102911/Is-Dugways-expansion-an-alien-concept.html*.

Beckley, Timothy Green. *The Shaver Mystery and the Inner Earth*. Mokelumne, Calif.: Mokelumne Hill Press, 1985.

Begich, Dr. Nick, and Jeane Manning. "HAARP: Vandalism in the Sky?" *Nexus Magazine* 3, No. 1, December 1995–January 1996.

Berlitz Charles, and William L. Moore. *The Philadelphia Experiment*. London: Granada Publishing Ltd., 1980.

Bishop, Greg. "Dulce Base Was/Is Real." UFOMystic. com, September 24, 2010. *www.ufomystic.com/2010/ 09/24/dulce-base-was-is-real/*.

———. "Official name for Dulce, New Mexico underground base disclosed!!" UFOMystic.com, September 27, 2010. *www.ufomystic.com/2010/09/27/ official-name-for-dulce-new-mexico-underground-base-disclosed/*.

———. *Project Beta*. New York: Paraview-Pocket Books, 2005.

———. "Report: Dulce Underground Base Conference." UFOMystic.com, March 29, 2009. *www.ufomystic.com/2009/03/29/ report-dulce-underground-base-conference/*.

Bishop III, Jason. "The Dulce Base." *www.subversive element.com/DulceBishop2.html*.

Bragalia, Anthony. "Deep Secrets of a UFO Think Tank Exposed." The UFO Iconoclast(s), July 27, 2009. *ufocon.blogspot.com/2009_07_26_archive.html*.

———. "Is this where alien bodies are stored? The secrets of a place called Dugway." The UFO Iconoclast(s), February 7, 2011. *ufocon.blogspot. com2011/02/is-this-where-alien-bodies-are-stored.html*.

Bruni, Georgina. *You Can't Tell the People*. London: Macmillan, 2001.

"Bulldog Jack [later re-named Alias Bulldog Drummond]." IMDB.com. *www.imdb.com/title/tt0024933/*.

"Camp Hero." *www.subversiveelement.com/camphero.html*.

Campbell, Glenn. "Bob Lazar Claims to Have Worked with Alien Craft at 'Area S-4' in Nevada." *www.ufomind.com/area51/people/lazar/*, January 2000.

Caribbean Primate Research Center. *cprc.rcm.upr.edu/*.

"Christian Pacifists Challenge Pine Gap in Court." Scoop World, October 6, 2006. *www.scoop.co.nz/stories/WO0610/S00120.htm*.

Cianciosi, Scott. "The Sheep Incident." Damn Interesting, March 17, 2008. *www.damninteresting.com/the-sheep-incident*.

Clarke, David. "The Secret Files: The Cosford Incident." Flying Saucery Presents...The Real UFO Project, 2005. *www.uk-ufo.org/condign/secfilcosf2.htm*.

"Cold War Bunkers and Radar Stations." TheTimeChamber, 2007. *www.thetimechamber.co.uk/sites/Civil/Rotor.php*.

Committee on Veterans' Affairs. *Is Military Research Hazardous to Veterans Health? Lessons Spanning Half a Century*. Staff Report, December 8, 1994.

Cooper, Steve. "Was HAARP Missile Defense Test behind Massive Bird Deaths?" The Conservative Monster.com, January 5, 2011. *theconservativemonster.com/2011/01/05/was-haarp-missile-defense-test-behind-massive-bird-deaths.aspx*.

Covington, John. "Fugos: Japanese Balloon Bombs of WWII." *www.seanet.com/~johnco/fugo.htm*, December 30, 2010.

"The Crown of St. Stephen." Jimmy Carter Library & Museum. *www.jimmycarterlibrary.gov/museum/crown.phtml*.

Darlington, David. *Area 51: The Dreamland Chronicles*. New York: Henry Holt, 1998.

Davidson, Lee. "Mysterious Deaths: Ex-soldier links horses' malady in 1976 to his poor health." *Deseret News*, August 28, 2005. *www.deseretnews.com/article/600158926/Mysterious-deaths-Ex-soldier-links-horses-malady-in-1976-to-his-poor-health.html*.

Davidson, Michael, and Michael C. Ruppert. "A Career in Microbiology can be Harmful to Your Health." FromTheWilderness.com, February 14, 2002. *www.fromthewilderness.com/free/ww3/02_14_02_microbio.html*.

Davis, Eric W. "Teleportation Physics Study." Warp Drive Metrics, for the Air Force Research Laboratory, Air Force Materiel Command, Edwards Air Force Base, November 25, 2003.

"Death Line [U.S. title, Raw Meat]." IMDB.com. *www.imdb.com/title/tt0068458/*, 2001.

Department of Defense, Office of the Secretary. "Conduct on the Pentagon Reservation." *www.fas.org/sgp/news/2007/05/fr052507.html*, May 25, 2007.

"Did HAARP Kill Thousands of Birds and Fish Simultaneously Across Country?" Now the End Begins, 2010. *www.nowtheendbegins.com/pages/unexplained/did-HAARP-kill-thousands-of-brids-and-fish.htm*.

Dodd, Tony. *Alien Investigator*. London: Headline, 1999.

Dolan, Richard. "Musings on a Secret Space Program." Para-News.info, June 6, 2010. *richardthomasblogger.blogspot.com/2010/06/guest-article-by-richard-dolan.html*.

"'Doomsday' Seed Bank to be Built." *BBC News*, January 12, 2006. *news.bbc.co.uk/2/hi/science/nature/4605398.stm*.

"Doomsday Vault Begins Deep Freeze." *BBC News*, November 16, 2007. *news.bbc.co.uk/2/hi/science/nature/7097052.stm*.

Downes, Jonathan. *The Island of Paradise*. Woolsery, United Kingdom: CFZ Press, 2008.

———. *Monster Hunter*. Woolsery, United Kingdom: CFZ Press, 2004.

Doyle, Patricia. "More Dead Top Microbiologist Scientists." Rense.com, January 29, 2004. *www.rense.com/general48/moredead.htm*.

Dreamland Resort. *www.dreamlandresort.com/*, February 1, 2011.

"Dr. David Kelly." *dr-david-kelly.blogspot.com/*, October 31, 2010.

"Dr. Nick Begich." Earthpulse.com, 2011. *www.earthpulse.com/src/category.asp?catid=13*.

"Dr. Strangelove, or: How I Learned to Stop Worrying and Love the Bomb." IMDB.com. *www.imdb.com/title/tt0057012/*.

Dsouza, Larkins. "SR91 Aurora Aircraft." Defence Aviation, June 26, 2007. *www.defenceaviation.com/2007/06/sr-91-aurora-aircraft.html*.

Duffy, Michael. "Weapons of War—Poison Gas." Firstworldwar.com, August 22, 2009. *www.firstworldwar.com/weaponry/gas.htm*.

"Dugway Genesis Team Ready To Ship Samples To Houston." Space Daily, October 1, 2004. *www.space-daily.com/news/genesis-04t.html*.

"Dugway Proving Ground." *www.dugway.army.mil/*.

"Dugway Proving Ground Survivors." *www.project-112 shad-fdn.com/*.

"Dugway says lockdown caused by 'serious mishandling' of nerve agent." KSL.com, January 27, 2011. *www.ksl.com/?sid=14157393&nid=148*.

"Dulce." Monstrous.com. *http://aliens.monstrous.com/dulce.htm*.

"Dulce Underground Base." *www.ufocasebook.com/dulce.html*.

"The Dulce Underworld." *www.subversiveelement.com/dulce_index.html*.

Dume, Belle. "Elements 115 and 113 Discovered in Dubna." Physicsworld.com, February 3, 2004. *physicsworld.com/cws/article/news/18954*.

"Edward Teller, Ph.D." Academy of Achievement, October 14, 2010. *www.achievement.org/autodoc/page/tel0bio-1*.

"Element 115—Bob Lazar Was Right." *area51.ablog.ro/2007-04-30/element-115-bob-lazar-was-right.html*, April 30, 2007.

Elliott, S.M. "Hoaxes from Space Part I: Bob Lazar." *Swallowing the Camel*, August 31, 2009. *swallowingthecamel.blogspot.com/2009/08/hoaxes-from-space-part-i-bob-lazar.html*.

England, Terry. "LA Man Joins the Jet Set—at 200 Miles an Hour." *Los Alamos Monitor*, June 27, 1982.

Erickson, Steve. "U.S. Army Dugway Proving Ground: Basin for Bio-Testing." *www.project-112shad-fdn.com/erickson.htm*, May 16, 2003.

Evans, Michael. "Porton Down guinea-pigs get apology." *Sunday Times*, January 18, 2008.

"Experts Say Japan Has 300 Years' Oil." *New York Times*, February 21, 1922. *query.nytimes.com/mem/archive-free/pdf?res=F10A1EF9395D14738DDDA80A94DA405B828EF1D3*.

Farrell, Joseph P. *Secrets of the Unified Field*. Kempton, Ill.: Adventures Unlimited Press, 2008.

"Federal Government Closing off all Caves across Country." December 21 2012.com Forum, March 1, 2011. *www.december212012.com/phpBB2/viewtopic.php?f=5&t=10888*.

Figueroa, William. "History of Puerto Rico." Sol Boricua. *www.solboricua.com/history.htm*.

"The Fly (1958)." IMDB.com. *www.imdb.com/title/tt0051622/*.

"Fort Detrick: A Sustainable Community of Excellence." U.S. Army, 2011. *www.detrick.army.mil/*.

"Fort Knox Bullion Depository." GlobalSecurity.org. *www.globalsecurity.org/military/facility/fort-knox-depository.htm*.

Friedman, Stanton T. "The Bob Lazar Fraud." StantonFriedman.com, December 15, 1997. *www.stantonfriedman.com/index.php?ptp=articles&fdt=1997.12.15*.

Frost, Cassandra "Sandy." "Remote Viewing Underground UFO Bases." Rense.com, November 28, 2005. *www.rense.com/general68/remm.htm*.

"Gasbuggy Nuclear Test Site." The Center for Land Use Interpretation. *http://ludb.clui.org/ex/i/NM3130/*.

"Genesis." NASA.gov, November 23, 2007. *www.nasa .gov/mission_pages/genesis/main/index.html*.

Genzlinger, Anna Lykins. *The Jessup Dimension*. Clarksburg, W.Va.: Saucerian Press, 1981.

Gerig, Bruce L. "Searching for Noah's Ark." *epistle.us/ articles/noah.html*, 2003.

Goldstein, Steve. "'Undisclosed Location' Disclosed." *The Boston Globe*, July 20, 2004. *www.boston.com/news/ nation/articles/2004/07/20undisclosed_location_disclosed/*.

"Goldwater, Barry Morris, (1909-1998)." Biographical Directory of the United States Congress. *bioguide. congress.gov/scripts/biodisplay.pl?index=G000267*.

Goldwater, Senator Barry. Letter to Shlomo Arnon, March 28, 1975. Reproduced in Good, Timothy, *Above Top Secret*, London: Sidgwick & Jackson, 1987.

Good, Timothy. *Above Top Secret*. London: Sidgwick & Jackson, 1987.

———. *Alien Base*. London: Arrow, 1999.

———. *Alien Liaison*. London: Century, 1991.

Goodrick-Clarke, Nicholas. *Black Sun*. New York: New York University Press, 2002.

———. *The Occult Roots of Nazism*. Wellingborough, England: The Aquarian Press, 1985.

Goodwin, Liz. "Japan's Earthquake Shifted Balance of the Planet." Yahoo! News, March 14, 2011. *news.yahoo. com/s/yblog_thelookout/20110314/ ts_yblog_thelookout/japans-earthquake-shifted-balance- of-the-planet*.

Guest, E.A. "The Other Paradigm." *Fate*, April 2005.

HAARP. *haarp.net/*.

Haines, Gerald K. "A Die-Hard Issue: CIA's Role in the Study of UFOs, 1947–90." *Intelligence and National Security* 14, No. 2 (Summer 1999).

"Haiti." U.S. Army Geospacial Center. *www.agc.army. mil/Haiti/index.html*.

"Haiti Could Have Larger Oil Reserves Than Venezuela." World Oil Online, January 27, 2010. *www.worldoil. com/Haiti_could_have_larger_oil_reserves_than_ Venezuela.html*.

"Haiti Earthquake Conspiracy, HAARP, EISCAT Experiments on January 12, 2010." Ahrcanum, January 14, 2010. *ahrcanum.wordpress.com/2010/01/14/ haiti-earthquake-conspiracy-haarp-eiscat/*.

Hamilton III, William. *Cosmic Top Secret*. New Brunswick, New Jersey: Inner Light, 1991.

Harding, Thomas. "Chinese Nuclear Submarine Base." *The Telegraph*, May 1, 2008. *www.telegraph.co.uk/ news/worldnews/asia/china/1917167/Chinese-nuclear- submarine-base.html*.

Harris, Paul. "Apocalypse Now? Mystery Bird Deaths Hit Louisiana." *Guardian*, January 4, 2011.

Head, Mike. "Australian court quashes convictions of protesters for entering US spy base." World Socialist Web Site, April 7, 2008. *www.wsws.org/articles/2008/ apr2008/pine-a07.shtml*.

Heffernan, Mike. "Ghosts of the London Underground." Unexplained Mysteries, September 12, 2008. *www.unexplained-mysteries.com/column. php?id=135129*.

Hickey, Jim. "Underground Bunkers Are Big Business." *ABC News*, March 24, 2011. *abcnews.go.com/Business/underground-bunkers-big-business/story?id=13212546*.

The High Frequency Active Auroral Research Program, HAARP. *www.haarp.alaska.edu/*, July 21, 2010.

Hirsch, Robert. "Peaking of World Oil Production: Impacts, Mitigation, and Risk Management." National Energy Technology Laboratory, February 2005. *www.netl.doe.gov/publications/others/pdf/Oil_Peaking_NETL.pdf*.

"History of Puerto Rico." *welcome.topuertorico.org/history.shtml*.

Holy Bible, English Standard Version. Wheaton, Ill.: Crossway Books, 2011.

"Horizon Lunar Outpost." Encyclopedia Astronautica. *www.astronautix.com/craft/hortpost.htm*.

Huff, Gene. "The Lazar Synopsis." *www.ufo.it/testi/lazar.htm*, March 12, 1995.

"I saw Structures on the Moon (Karl Wolfe)." *www.ufo-casebook.com/moonstructures.html*.

"Ingo Swann Gets Feedback Regarding Naked Men on the Moon." Alien Zoo Secret Archives, April 27, 2000. *http://archive.alienzoo.com/conspiracytheory/ingo-swann.html*.

"Ingo Swann-Penetration The moon remotely viewed." Abovetopsecret.com, September 28, 2009. *www.abovetopsecret.com/forum/thread505569/pg1*.

"Inside Area 51." *The Las Vegas Review-Journal*. *www.reviewjournal.com/webextras/area51/*.

"Interview Larry Warren, Rendlesham Forest UFO Case Key Witness." Abovetopsecret.com, February 15, 2009. *video.abovetopsecret.com/video3153/Interview_Larry_Warren_Rendlesham_Forest_UFO_case_key_witness./*.

"Invasion Earth." IMDB.com. *www.imdb.com/title/tt0140743/*.

"Japan." Wikipedia. *en.wikipedia.org/wiki/Global_strategic_petroleum_reserves#Japan*.

"Japanese Fugo Bombing Balloons." Marshall Stelzriede's Wartime Story: The Experiences of a B-17 Navigator During World War II. *www.stelzriede.com/ms/html/mshwfugo.htm*.

Jessup, Morris. *The Case for the UFO*. New York: Bantam, 1955.

Johnson, Bruce. "Holocaust Gold Taints the Vatican." *Sunday Telegraph*, July 27, 1997.

Jones, Andrew Zimmerman. "What is Unified Field Theory?" About.com: Physics. *physics.about.com/od/quantumphysics/f/uft.htm*.

Jones, Marie D. *2013: The End of Days or a New Beginning?* Pompton Plains, New Jersey: New Page Books, 2008.

Jordan, Lara Jakes. "Senator: Anthrax not 1 man's work." *Denver Post*, September 18, 2008. *www.denverpost.com/ci_10492103?source=pkg*.

"Kapustin Yar." *www.spyflight.co.uk/yar.htm*, February 15, 2009.

Kilgallen, Dorothy. "Flying Saucer News." *Los Angeles Examiner*, May 23, 1955.

Knapp, George. "Bob Lazar: The Man Behind Area 51." 8NewsNow.com. *www.8newsnow.com/story/3369879/ bob-lazar-the-man-behind-area-51*.

Kossov, Igor. "Cheney's 'Undisclosed Location' Revealed?" *CBS News*, May 18, 2009. *www.cbsnews.com/8301-503544_162-5022777-503544.html*.

"Kuji Media Corporation: The History of a Computer Hacker." *www.kujimedia.com/*, 2007.

Lederer, Adam. "Project Wagon Wheel: A Nuclear Plowshare for Wyoming." Annals of Wyoming, Summer 1998. *uwacadweb.uwyo.edu/robertshistory/ project_wagon_wheel.htm*.

Leonard, George. *Somebody Else Is on the Moon*. New York: Pocket, 1977.

"London Underground Ghosts." BBC. *www.bbc.co.uk/ dna/h2g2/alabaster/A673391*.

"London Underground Ghosts." Ghost-Story.co.uk, May 15, 2010. *www.ghost-story.co.uk/stories/ londonundergoundghosts.html*.

Lowe, Keith. *Tunnel Vision*. London: Arrow, 2001.

Lynn, Katalin Kadar. "The Return of the Crown of St. Stephen and its Subsequent Impact on the Carter Administration." Highbeam Research, June 22, 2000. *www.highbeam.com/doc/1G1-63126015.html*.

MacDonald, G. Jeffrey. "Does Maya Calendar Predict 2012 Apocalypse?" *USA Today*, March 27, 2007. *www.usatoday.com/tech/science/2007-03-27-maya-2012_N.htm*.

Marchetti, Victor. "How the CIA Views the UFO Phenomenon." *Second Look* 1, No. 7 (May 1979).

Martín, Jorge. "UFOs and Aliens in the Caribbean." IRAAP, 2000. *www.iraap.org/Martin/UFOsandAliens.htm*.

Meek, James Gordon. "FBI was told to blame Anthrax scare on Al Qaeda by White House Officials." *New York Daily News*, August 2, 2008. *www.nydailynews. com/news/national/2008/08/02/2008-08-02_fbi_wastold_ to_blame_anthrax_scare_on_a.html*.

"Missing nerve agent led to Dugway lockdown." UPI.com, January 27, 2011. *www.upi.com/Top_News/US/ 2011/01/27/Missing-nerve-agent-led-to-Dugway-lockdown/ UPI-34971296139839/*.

"MI6 payouts over secret LSD tests." *BBC News*, February 24, 2006. *http://news.bbc.co.uk/2/hi/uk_ news/4745748.stm*.

"MoD's Porton Down and Secret Experiments." *Eye Spy* magazine. *www.eyespymag.com/features/porton.html*.

"Montauk Project." *www.bibliotecapleyades.net/montauk/ esp_montauk.htm*.

"The Montauk Project." *www.theironskeptic.com/articles/ montauk/montauk.htm*.

Moon, Peter, and Preston B. Nichols. *The Montauk Project: Experiment in Time*. New York: Sky Books, 1992.

Moore, William L. *The Philadelphia Experiment: Update*. Burbank, Calif.: William L. Moore Publications, 1984.

"Nancy Lieder: Zetatalk and the Nibiru Connection." Conquer 2012, June 29, 2010. *www.conquer2012.com- nancy-lieder-zetatalk-and-the-nibiru-theory-connection/*.

Nelson, Wade H. "Nuclear Explosion Shook Farmington." *www.wadenelson.com/gasbuggy.html*, 1999.

"Nerve gas inquest to be reopened." *BBC News*, November 18, 2002. *news.bbc.co.uk/2/hi/uk_news/england/2488473.stm.*

Oaks, Marsha. "Paranormal Entertainment." *Atlantis Rising*, May 1, 2008. *atlantisrisingmagazine.com/2008/05/01/paranormal-entertainment/.*

Passantino, Jonathan. "Biden Reveals Location of Secret VP Bunker." *Fox News*, May 18, 2009. *www.foxnews.com/politics/2009/05/18/biden-reveals-location-secret-vp-bunker/.*

Patton, Phil. *Dreamland: Travels Inside the Secret World of Roswell and Area 51.* New York: Random House, 1999.

Phayer, Michael. *The Catholic Church and the Holocaust, 1939–1965.* Bloomington, Ind.: Indiana University Press, 2001.

"The Philadelphia Experiment." IMDB.com. *www.imdb.com/title/tt0087910/.*

Pike, John. "Mystery Aircraft: Aurora/Senior Citizen." FAS.org, July 24, 1998. *www.fas.org/irp/mystery/aurora.htm.*

———. "Pine Gap, Australia." FAS.org, October 20, 1999. *www.fas.org/irp/facility/pine_gap.htm.*

———. "Site-R Raven Rock Alternate Joint Communications Center (AJCC)." FAS.org. *www.fas.org/nuke/guide/usa/c3i/raven_rock.htm.*

"Pilot may have caused fatal plane crash by switching to empty fuel tank." *Daily Mail*, August 3, 2007. *www.dailymail.co.uk/news/article-471827/Pilot-caused-fatal-plane-crash-switching-fuel-tank.html.*

"Pine Gap, Australian 'Area 51.'" *www.bibliotecapleyades.net/esp_sociopol_pinegap.htm*, 2011.

Pope, Nick. *Operation Thunder Child*. London: Simon & Schuster, 1999.

———. "The Cosford Incident." NickPope.net. *www.nickpope.net/cosford-incident.htm*.

"Porton Down." Ministry of Defence, The National Archives. *http://webarchive.nationalarchives.gov.uk/+/http://www.mod.uk/DefenceInternet/AboutDefence/WhatWeDo/HealthandSafety/PortonDownVolunteers/PortonDown.htm*.

Potter, Paul E. "Bob Lazar's Gravity Generator." *www.gravitywarpdrive.com/Gravity_Generator.htm*, April 10, 2000.

Preusz, Jared. "Mislabeled vial of nerve agent responsible for Dugway lockdown." Fox13Now.com, January 27, 2011. *www.fox13now.com/news/local/kstu-dugway-lockdown,0,4633684.story*.

"Project Gasbuggy." *www.atomictourist.com/gasbug.htm*.

"Puerto Rico History." ElYunque.com. *www.elyunque.com/history.html*.

Quayle, Steve. "List of Dead Scientists." *www.stevequayle.com/index1.html*, 2011.

Randles, Jenny. *From out of the Blue*. New Brunswick, New Jersey: Inner Light-Global Communications, 1991.

———. *UFO Crash Landing?* London: Blandford, 1998.

Ravenscroft, Trevor. *The Spear of Destiny*. Newburyport, Mass.: Weiser Books, 1982.

"Raymond A. Palmer." Absolute Astronomy. *www.absoluteastronomy.com/topics/Raymond_A._Palmer*.

"Raymond A. Palmer—Summary Bibliography." ISFDB. *www.isfdb.org/cgi-bin/ea.cgi?Raymond_A._Palmer*.

Redfern, Nick. *Body Snatchers in the Desert*. New York: Paraview-Pocket Books, 2005.

———. *Cosmic Crashes*. London: Simon & Schuster, 2001.

———. "The Flying Saucer that Never Was." In *Intermediate States: The Anomalist 13*. San Antonio, Texas: Anomalist Books, 2007.

———. "In Search of the Chupacabras." *Fate* 58, No. 1 (2005).

———. Interview with Frank Wiley, June 3, 2004.

———. Interview with Ministry of Defense source referred to Redfern by Nick Pope, March 27, 1998.

———. Interview with Mac Tonnies, July 7, 2009.

———. "Is This Really Noah's Ice Tomb?" *Western Daily Press*, July 3, 2001.

———. *London's Underground Wonders*. Dallas, Texas: Self-published, 2007.

———. "Manipulating the Crashed UFO Scene." The UFO Iconoclast(s), June 2, 2009. *ufocon.blogspot.com/2009/06/manipulating-crashed-ufo-scene-by-nick.html*.

———. *Memoirs of a Monster Hunter*. Pompton Plains, New Jersey: New Page Books, 2007.

———. *The NASA Conspiracies*. Pompton Plains, New Jersey: New Page Books, 2010.

———. "Rendlesham: About Those Missing Files." Mysterious Universe, March 16, 2011. *mysteriousuniverse.org/2011/03/rendlesham-about-those-missing-files/*.

———. "The Riddle of Hangar 18." *Planet on Sunday*, December 4, 1999.

———. "UFOs on Radar—Remarkable New Data!" *UFO Magazine*, January/February, 2000.

Redfern, Nick, and Jonathan Downes. *Weird War Tales*. Woolsery, United Kingdom: CFZ Press, 2001.

"Reign of Fire." IMDB.com. *www.imdb.com/title/ tt0253556/*.

Rich, Ben R., and Leo Janos. *Skunk Works: A Personal Memoir of My Years at Lockheed*. Boston, Mass.: Little, Brown, 1996.

Roberts, Andy. *UFO Down?* Woolsery, United Kingdom: Fortean Words, 2010.

Ronson, John. "Gary McKinnon: Pentagon hacker's worst nightmare comes true." *Guardian*, August 1, 2009. *www.guardian.co.uk/world/2009/aug/01/ gary-mckinnon-extradition-nightmare*.

Roosevelt Roads. *www.roosey-roads.com/*, 2009.

"Roosevelt Roads Naval Station." GlobalSecurity.org. *www. globalsecurity.org/military/facility/roosevelt-roads.htm*.

Rose, Bill. "America's Secret Space Program...and the Super Valkyrie." *www.bibliotecapleyades.net/ciencia/ ciencia_flyingobjects53.htm*, June 21, 2004.

"Rotor Radar System." *www.radarpages.co.uk/mob/rotor/ rotorarticle1.htm*, September 29, 1998.

Royal Air Force. *Royal Air Force Provost & Security Services Brochure*. London: Her Majesty's Stationery Office, 1994.

Ryan, Bill, and Kerry Cassidy. "A Letter from a Norwegian Politician." *www.projectcamelot.org/norway.html*, 2010.

Salla, Dr. Michael. "The Dulce Report." Exopolitics.org, September 25, 2003. *www.exopolitics.org/dulce-report.htm*.

Scahill, Jeremy. *Blackwater: The Rise of the World's Most Powerful Mercenary*. New York: Army Nation Books, 2007.

———. "Will Blackwater Be Kicked out of Iraq After Recent Bloodbath?" *The Nation*, September 28, 2007.

Schnabel, Jim. *Remote Viewers*. New York: Dell Publishing, 1997.

Scott, Irena. "WPAFB 'Aliens,' Little Green Men History, First On-Base View of Secured Interview." *www.youtube.com/watch?v=mcxGcLLxjyY*, February 11, 2007.

Scott, Irena, and William E. Jones. "The Little Green Men of Wright-Patt." MUFON of Ohio, 2010. *www.mufonohio.com/greenmen.html*.

"Secret Sanya—China's New Nuclear Naval Base Revealed." World Defence Network, Pakistan Defence, April 21, 2008. *www.defence.pk/forums/strategic-geopolitical-issues/11741-secret-sanya-chinas-new-nuclear-naval-base-revealed.html*.

"Senators Condemn Mystery Spy Project." MSNBC, December 8, 2004. *www.msnbc.msn.com/id/6682352/ns/us_news-security/*.

Shapiro, Joshua. "The Montauk Project and the Philadelphia Experiment." *www.v-j-enterprises.com/montauk.html*.

"The Shaver Mystery and the Truth about Earth's Past." *BBC News*, January 24, 2002. *www.bbc.co.uk/dna/h2g2/A676244*.

Simpson, George Eaton, and Neal R. Burger. *Thin Air*. New York: Dell, 1977.

Skehan, Craig. "Pine Gap gears for war with eye on Iraq." SMH.com.au, September 30, 2002. *www.smh. com.au/articles/2002/09/29/1033283389127.html*.

Sky, Eden. "20 Questions on 2012." *www.13moon.com/ prophecy%20page.htm#nav4*, 2009.

Slany, William Z., and Stuart Eizenstat. "U.S. and Allied Wartime and Postwar Relations and Negotiations with Argentina, Portugal, Spain, Sweden, and Turkey on Looted Gold and German External Assets and U.S. Concerns about the Fate of the Wartime Ustasha Treasury." Washington, D.C.: U.S. Government Printing Office, 1998. *www.state.gov/www/ policy_remarks/1998/980602_eizenstat_nazigld.html*.

Smith, Charles R. "UFO Secrets." Newsmax.com, January 15, 2004. *http://archive.newsmax.com/archives/ articles/2004/1/14/222343.shtml*.

Smith, Mark S. "West Wing Disappears Behind Noisy Construction Job." Sign on San Diego, April 4, 2011. *www.signonsandiego.com/news/2011/apr/04/ west-wing-disappears-behind-noisy-construction-job/*.

The Smithsonian Institution. *www.si.edu/*.

Soames, Nicholas, Defense Minister. Report to Martin Redmond, Member of Parliament, October 27, 1996.

Steiger, Brad. *Monsters among Us*. New York: Berkley Books, 1989.

Steiger, Brad, Sherry Steiger, and Al Bielek. *The Philadelphia Experiment and Other UFO Conspiracies*. New Brunswick, New Jersey: Inner Light, 1990.

"Strange Lights Appear in the Sky above Utah County." *www.abc4.com/content/news/slc/story/Strange-lights-appear-in-the-sky-above-Utah-County/Wo5f7K0sTEi6_tM5q_-hxg.cspx*, January 27, 2011.

Stringfield, Leonard. *Situation Red: The UFO Siege.* London: Sphere Books, Ltd., 1978.

———. *The UFO Crash/Retrieval Syndrome.* Seguin, Texas: The Mutual UFO Network, January 1980.

———. *UFO Crash/Retrievals: Amassing the Evidence.* Cincinnati, Ohio: published privately, June 1982.

———. *UFO Crash/Retrievals: The Inner Sanctum.* Cincinnati, Ohio: published privately, July 1991.

Svalbard Global Seed Vault. *www.nordgen.org/sgsv/.*

"Svalbard Global Seed Vault." *www.regjeringen.no/en/dep/lmd/campain/svalbard-global-seed-vault.html*, 2011.

Swann, Ingo. *Penetration.* Rapid City, S.D.: Ingo Swann Books, 1998.

Tanter, Richard. "Pine Gap protests—historical."*gc.nautilus.org/Nautilus/australia/australian-defence-facilities/pine-gap/pine-gap-protests/protests-hist/*, April 6, 2008.

Timmerman, Kenneth R. "Inside Russia's Magic Mountain." WorldNetDaily, June 6, 2000. *www.wnd.com/?pageId=4137.*

Tonnies, Mac. Posthuman Blues, December 27, 2006. *posthumanblues.blogspot.com/2006/12/cryptoterrestrial-hypothesis-has-met.html.*

———. Posthuman Blues, April 16, 2006. *http://posthuman-blues.blogspot.com/2006/04/of-course-cryptoterrestrials-dont.html.*

"The Top Secret U.S. Military Space Program. Is the Future Already Here?" Abovetopsecret.com, January, 28, 2008. *www.abovetopsecret.com/forum/thread329997/pg1*.

"Toxicology: Sheep and the Army." *Time*, April 5, 1968.

Tuttle, Rich. "Senators Comments Suggest Evidence of Secret Space Program." *Aviation Week*, December 13, 2004. *www.aviationweek.com/aw/generic/story_generic.jsp?channel=aerospacedaily&id=news/SECRET12134.xml*.

Tyler, Captain Paul. *Intensity Conflict and Modern Technology*. Edited by Lt. Col. David J. Dean. Montgomery, Ala.: Air University Press, June 1986.

Underground History. *underground-history.co.uk/front.php*.

United States Air Force. "Air Force 2025." *www.fas.org/spp/military/docops/usaf/2025/*, declassified June 17, 1996.

———. "Unidentified Flying Objects—Project Blue Book." The U.S. National Archives and Records Administration, January 14, 1985. *www.archives.gov/foia/ufos.html*.

United States Army. "Project Horizon Report: Volume I, Summary and Supporting Considerations." *www.history.army.mil/faq/horizon/Horizon_V1.pdf*, June 9, 1959.

———. "Project Horizon Report: Volume II, Technical Considerations & Plans." *www.history.army.mil/faq/horizon/Horizon_V2.pdf*, June 9, 1959.

United States Navy. "Information Sheet: Philadelphia Experiment." *www.history.navy.mil/faqs/faq21-2.htm*, September 8, 1996.

———. "The Philadelphia Experiment." *www.history.navy.mil/faqs/faq21-1.htm*, November 28, 2000.

U.S. Department of Defense. "DoD News Briefing: Secretary of Defense William S. Cohen." *www.defense.gov/transcripts/transcript.aspx?transcriptid=674*, April 28, 1997.

U.S. Fish & Wildlife Service. "White-Nose Syndrome: Something is Killing our Bats." *www.fws.gov/whitenosesyndrome/*, April 19, 2011.

"U.S. Nukes can be Adapted for use Against Enemy: Bush." *The Times of India*, May 25, 2003. */articles.timesofindia.indiatimes.com/2003-05-25/us/27265260_1_nuclear-security-nuclear-terrorism-bruce-g-blair*.

U.S. Senate Permanent Sub-Committee on Investigations. "Security in Cyberspace." *www.fas.org/irp/congress/1996_hr/s960605b.htm*, June 5, 1996.

Van Kampen, K.R. "Effects of nerve gas poisoning in sheep in Skull Valley, Utah." *Journal of the American Veterinary Medical Association* 156, No. 8 (April 15, 1970).

"Vatican and Nazi Gold." *mprofaca.cro.net/vatigold.html*.

"Vatican Asks Court, U.S. Government to Dismiss Lawsuit over Nazi Gold." *American Atheists*, No. 847 (November 27, 2000).

"Vatican Bank Sued Over Nazi Gold." Easton & Levy Press Release. *www.remnantofgod.org/art52.htm*, January 21, 2000.

Vergano, Dan. "Air Force report calls for $7.5M to study psychic teleportation." *USA Today*, November 5, 2004. *www.usatoday.com/tech/news/2004-11-05-teleportation_x.htm*.

"Vladimir Pasechnik." *Guardian*, November 28, 2001. *www.guardian.co.uk/news/2001/nov/28/guardianobituaries.highereducation*.

"Vladimir Pasechnik." *The Telegraph*, November 29, 2001. *www.telegraph.co.uk/news/obituaries/1363752/Vladimir-Pasechnik.html*.

Wagner, Stephen. "Is Nibiru Approaching?" About.com: Paranormal Phenomena. *aranormal.about.com/od/zsitchinniburu/a/Is-Nibiru-Approaching.htm*.

———. "What's on the Far Side of the Moon?" About.com: Paranormal Phenomena, January 15, 2007. *paranormal.about.com/od/lunaranomalies/a/aa011507_2.htm*.

Ward, Mark. "History Repeats for Former Hacker." *BBC News*, May 11, 2006. *news.bbc.co.uk/2/hi/technology/4761985.stm*.

Warren, Larry, and Peter Robbins. *Left at East Gate*. New York: Cosimo, 2005.

Watts, Peter. "London's Underground History." TimeOut London: The Big Smoke, April 17, 2007. *www.timeout.com/london/big-smoke/features/2814/London_Underground-s_history.html*.

Woolf, Jim. "Feds finally admit that nerve agent was found near 1968 sheep kill." *Salt Lake Tribune*, January 2, 1998.

INDEX

N

O

P

R

S